Before You Go Overseas

The 21 Essentials to International Travel

by

Derek Cooper

THOMAS INSTITUTE PRESS

Thomas Institute Press
Blooming Glen, Pennsylvania

Published in the United States and the United Kingdom

ISBN 978-1-63683-047-6 (pbk.)
ISBN 978-1-63683-936-9 (ebk.)

Printed in the United States of America

Other Books by Derek Cooper

Christianity and New Religious Movements: An Introduction to the World's Newest Faiths

Commentary on Proverbs

Basics of Latin: A Grammar with Readings and Exercises from the Christian Tradition

Introduction to World Christian History

Sinners and Saints: The Real Story of Early Christianity

1-2 Samuel, 1-2 Kings, 1-2 Chronicles in the Reformation Commentary on Scripture

Twenty Questions That Shaped World Christian History

Exploring Church History

Christianity and World Religions: An Introduction to the World's Major Faiths

Thomas Manton: A Guided Tour of the Life and Thought of a Puritan Pastor

Unfollowers: Unlikely Lessons on Faith from Those Who Doubted

Hazardous: Committing to the Cost of Following Jesus

So You're Thinking about Going to Seminary

TABLE OF CONTENTS

Part 4: Finding Your Rhythm

Part 5: Mind, Body, and Spirit

Part 6: After Your Trip

Before You Go Overseas

CHAPTER 1
UNFORGETTABLE EXPERIENCES

Energy in Vietnam

From the moment I arrived in Ho Chi Minh City, Vietnam, I could feel the city's energy pulsating through my veins. The constant hum of motorbikes, the exotic shrines on every street corner, and the intoxicating aroma of local street food was overwhelming. But it was also invigorating. Almost as soon as we arrived at our hotel, I pulled aside a few intrepid travelers in the lobby and asked if they wanted to rent motorbikes and brave the city streets. "This is not part of the official tour," I cautioned, "and you all need to weigh the risks." A few minutes later several accepted my offer, and, before we knew it, we were on our way. Although we got separated from each other within the first thirty seconds, we eventually reunited and rendezvoused a few miles outside of the city center. For the next several hours, we had the time of our lives. We buzzed along back alleys, we darted through dirt roads, and we zoomed across narrow bridges.

Solemnity in Istanbul

We were enjoying our last day in Istanbul before flying down to the south of Turkey early the next morning. On a whim, I suggested that our group purchase tickets to a Whirling Dervishes ceremony scheduled later that night. Active for 800 years, the Mevlevi Order—commonly called the Whirling Dervishes—is based on the teachings of the famous author Rumi. As we learned that night, the ritual ceremony performed by the dervishes is deeply symbolic, with each action and article of clothing symbolizing the sacred. Almost as soon as the dervishes solemnly entered the intimate theater—wearing white robes with skirts that dance in midair and long conical hats that represent tombs—the rhythm of their movements was as mesmerizing as it was magical. For the next hour, a crowd of strangers became united as one people, enraptured by the steady beat of the kettle drum, the spellbinding resonance of the flute, and the gravity-defying gyrations of the dervishes. Despite having attended religious ceremonies of all kinds across the globe and across the spiritual divide, the dervishes ceremony was one of the most solemn of my life.

Figure 1.1 Whirling Dervishes Ceremony in Turkey

Sun in Copenhagen

It was early June in Denmark, and we were enjoying something highly unusual but glorious. We experienced a week of uninterrupted sun and warmth in a land where clouds and rain are always lurking in the distance. All of our days in Denmark were wonderful but one in particular stands out. After spending the morning boating through Copenhagen's narrow canals and enjoying lunch in the city's most photographed section—the picturesque New Harbour (*Nyhavn*)—we decided to pass the rest of our afternoon and evening at Tivoli Gardens, the world's second-oldest amusement park, conveniently located right in the heart of the city. Our time at Tivoli was one of those moments you wish you could freeze in time. After enjoying a splendid outdoor dinner where we feasted on fresh fish, exceptionally flavored fries, and a delicious blend of seasonable vegetables, we were excited to take advantage of another long summer night in Scandinavia when the sun seemingly refuses to set. Making the most of our time, we basked in the sunshine on a blanket as we watched an open-air theater performance, we tested our luck at carnival games as we strolled through the grounds, and we gobbled up delectable Danish treats from all the street vendors eager to fill our sugar-searching bellies.

Figure 1.2 Tivoli Gardens in Copenhagen, Denmark

Travel: The Difference between Knowing and Experiencing

There is nothing like travel. The precious experiences I shared represent mere snapshots of thousands of unforgettable moments I have been privileged to forge over the years. The memories I have made while traveling overseas shape me each and every day, in both large and small ways. I have learned more about the world and myself than I ever thought possible through the simple—yet multi-stepped—process of getting on a plane and venturing the unknown. To be sure, travel is not for everyone, and it is certainly a luxury that not all can afford, not all will tolerate, and not all may like. But for those who do travel, whether for leisure, work, school, or another reason altogether—and especially those who, like me, can't get enough of it—travel opens up the world in profound and indescribable ways and always leaves you itching for more. It's one thing to "know," for instance, that motorbikes are a common mode of transport in southeast Asian countries like Vietnam, but it is altogether different to "experience" being leg-to-leg and shoulder-to-shoulder with locals on motorbikes, to "experience" the rush of oncoming traffic from all directions, and to "experience" your stomach sinking into your socks as your motorbike unexpectedly dies while surrounded by thousands of other motorbikes zipping past you, clueless to your plight. These are experiences that last a lifetime. These are experiences that you will never forget.

Travel Unleashes the World

Travel is a most potent force. Few other things can so immediately and enduringly change opinions, expose deeply entrenched biases, uncover hidden talents, unmask both strengths and weaknesses, generate lifelong friends, learn about others, and create memories that push you through the hard times.

Travel is the world's most comprehensive training ground, the most intellectually stimulating classroom, and the most deeply illuminating retreat center. It's no wonder that soldiers are transported to faraway fields to be trained, that the educators of ancient Greece taught while walking through cities, and that pilgrims leave their countries when in search of God.

Travel is what we do all the time for almost any occasion— when we want to push ourselves and move beyond our comfort zones, when we want to learn and see what's really going on in the world, and when we want to unwind and unplug and distance ourselves from our daily routines.

In a word, travel has it all, encompassing everything from business to partying to research to service to vacation. Whether we recognize it or not, to live is to travel. It is what we do every day of our lives—in our minds, bodies, and souls—whether we are traveling to the mailbox to collect our bills, traveling to our memory banks to withdraw enough happy memories to endure another day of work, or traveling overseas to visit one of the wonders of the world.

Distilling Trips from the Past

Perhaps like you, travel has taught me more than I can possibly hope to convey. In fact, travel preserves my most precious and vulnerable memories as a human being. Almost daily—during a meal, upon smelling some fragrance, while sitting at my desk, after watching a movie, or when talking to a friend—something from one of my previous trips flashes through my mind like a bolt of lightning. Before I know it, I am transported back in time as if in a daydream, and I begin reliving what I experienced in the past and integrating it into what I am encountering in the present.

What have I learned most while traveling overseas? It's impossible to distill decades of travel experiences into a handful of pithy thoughts or sentences, but there are ongoing themes that I return to when I travel. As I reflect on my previous trips, as I revisit my journals, and as I dialogue with fellow pilgrims, I am able to pinpoint certain insights that travel has allowed me to make. To be sure, none of them are groundbreaking theories, and they are also quite subjective and personal, but they do represent deep truths that guide me like a spiritual compass.

Learning on Location and Traveling with Purpose

Among many other things, I have discovered that people

learn and grow best when on location, that is, when they are disconnected from their daily schedules and invited—and, on occasion, forced—to see the world from a different lens. I have observed the combination of travel, learning, and reflection to be life-changing, and I am excited to provide more opportunities for others to learn and experience the world in new ways through travel, beginning with you.

Before travelers like yourself ever step foot on a plane, however, I want them to spend time reflecting on their voyage, imagining what they will experience and imagining how that will shape them in their everyday lives. For this reason, weeks before your actual trip—or, at least, on the plane if you like to procrastinate—I recommend reading each of the chapters that follow. Altogether, these chapters represent twenty-five years of international travel experiences that I have been privileged to obtain across all corners of the globe. Having lived for different periods of time on four different continents and having led dozens of trips to all major world regions, I feel like a State Farm insurance commercial: "I know a thing or two because I've seen a thing or two."

I've experienced all the highs and lows that travel offers, and because I work with travelers going overseas for the first time, I am constantly reminded of how overwhelming travel can be. Therefore, I am acutely aware of all the steps travelers need to take from making a list of sites to visit to managing culture shock to maximizing your time to staying safe. When I began traveling the world, I was wet behind the ears and completely naïve. I learned all there is to know about travel the hard way. I made mistakes, I was "that guy" who looked out of place, and I fell for some of the oldest tricks in the let's-take-advantage-of-the-foreigner playbook. I didn't know a thing about booking an international flight, dealing with jet lag, purchasing insurance, devising contingency plans, thinking about the spiritual effects of travel, and much more.

This will not be the case for you. Whether this is your first trip overseas or you have been leading tours for years, this book contains useful information, personal anecdotes, time-tested techniques, data-driven guidelines, and travel insights from Andorra to Zimbabwe. As a certified travel agent and travel company owner, I will unlock the secrets of traveling well, happily, and in a manner that works best for you. An old African proverb says it takes a village to raise a child, but it takes insights from the whole world to make a traveler.

Conclusion

Upon completion of this book, I believe you will be physically, mentally, and spiritually ready for your journey, equipped for anything that comes your way—whether planned or unplanned—and excited about the journey lying ahead. And what is best, even after you have completed your trip, your voyage is just underway—with memories and experiences able to entertain, teach, and sustain for decades to come. As I like to say to my groups as I prepare them for trips, "travel like you mean it and enjoy the voyage that follows." There is nothing like travel. It's one of the greatest gifts that humans give or receive, truly a gift that keeps on giving by means of unforgettable experiences and priceless memories. As you prepare for your trip ahead and the voyage that follows, I wish you safe travels and bon voyage!

Reflection Questions

At the end of each chapter, I provide five questions for you to consider related to the theme and topics discussed. Be sure to respond to these questions, whether in the margins of this book or just quietly in your head, before moving on to the next chapter. Below are the questions for this chapter.

1. What is your emotional relationship to travel? Are you more indifferent, eager, or fearful?

2. What keeps you from traveling the most: money, physical limitations, busyness, or something else?

3. Everyone has a few, precious travel memories. While you might not have been to Vietnam or Turkey, what highlights can you recall from your own journeys? What made them memorable?

4. Why might maintaining a travel journal be a good habit?

5. What are you most hoping to get from reading this book?

CHAPTER 2
TRAVEL MINDSET

Budget Travel in Jordan

I was on the way to Petra, Jordan, one of the wonders of the ancient world and where part of *Indiana Jones and the Last Crusade* was filmed. We had stopped briefly at a tourist trap a few miles from the entrance and were chatting about the sweltering heat while several Jordanian men smoked shisha and drank mint tea. All of the sudden, the mood changed as four black SUVs arrived, all the same size and all with tinted windows and reinforced doors. The SUVs stopped directly in front of me, and I could see that all the drivers were Caucasians wearing suits, ties, and headsets. It was like a scene out of *Men in Black*.

After a moment, armed bodyguards emerged out of each suburban and quickly assessed their surroundings before a middle-aged man and woman wearing t-shirts, shorts, and sneakers exited from one of the suburban doors and entered the store. As they did so, my Jordanian guide gently placed his right hand in front of me, signaling that I should stay put, and told me that the man approaching was the president of some European country, probably going to Petra on holiday with his wife. Eventually, the scene calmed down, but everywhere I went in Petra, these two travelers were always remarkably close by (it's a small site, after all) and they were always surrounded by their bodyguards. They had no worries at all and toured Petra like royalty; everything was exquisitely arranged for them.

What Kind of Traveler Do You Want to Be?

"What kind of traveler do you want to be"? That is the first question I ask my travel groups when we prepare for a trip overseas. When I think about the travel experience that the couple above enjoyed in Petra, it was vastly different from my own. The president appeared in four bullet-proof SUVs with muscular bodyguards carefully monitoring each of his steps and probably returned to his five-star hotel with fine dining and impeccable service. By contrast, my last leg of the journey there took place on the back of a camel and my lunch that day consisted of two bananas and a granola bar, which is all the extra money I had allotted myself since the focus of that particular trip was research, not vacation.

Different Kinds of Travelers Create Different Kind of Experiences

Over the course of my journeys, I have witnessed every kind of traveler—ranging from honeymooners who never left the comforts of their hotels to nature lovers who never set foot in the touristy areas to pilgrims who never consumed anything more than rice and water. All travelers have their own reasons for traveling the way they do, but there's no denying that the kind of traveler you choose to be determines what kind of experience you will have.

Your Mindset Is Your Trip

I'm not just talking about money, though, to be sure, your budget certainly affects your overall travel experience. Instead, what I'm really referring to can variously be called "mindset," "mentality," "motivation," or "outlook." Will you adopt the mindset of a pilgrim on your trip? Will you assume the mentality of a vacationer? Or will you accept the outlook of a missionary? We have all heard the saying that "you reap with you sow," and, in many ways, it applies equally to travel in the sense that "you get out of a trip what you put into it."

Sociologists have long recognized that outlook influences outcome. The value we give to something determines how we handle it. Understood in this way, the purpose of your trip will determine what sort of mindset you will have to adopt. And, in turn, the mindset you adopt necessitates different planning, which impacts where you will stay, where you will go, what you will do, and how you will interact with the people and places you encounter.

Without a doubt, travel depends on numerous factors. Therefore, it would be naïve to expect that you can adopt the same mindset for every international destination. The place where you honeymoon or vacation, for instance, is going to feel vastly different from the place where you volunteer or enter a study-abroad program. Still, for the journey ahead, you will need to determine what kind of traveler you are so that you can be as prepared as possible.

15 Different Kinds of Travelers

I have identified approximately 15 kinds of travelers. (My list is not comprehensive.) Naturally, some travelers overlap and parallel each other, indicating that it's not unusual for a person to embody more than a single mindset. Honeymooners, after all, can simultaneously be vacationers, foodies, and nature lovers. At the same time, I have discerned that people's *primary* reasons for traveling overseas, though quite varied, tend to gravitate toward one mindset or mentality.

To say it differently, each of the kinds of travelers below represents a specific kind of tourism that individual tour agencies across the world cater to, each of which maintain their own unique brands, specialized clientele, and business models built on multi-million-dollar infrastructures. Here are those different mindsets, mentalities, and motivations arranged in no order.

(1) Vacationers
They are, classically, those who are part of a group tour and spend time only with fellow vacationers. They stick to historic

landmarks, museums, private transportation, touristy restaurants, and four-star hotels. In a word, they are sightseers who want to take the comforts of home to their international destination.

(2) Explorers
These are perhaps the most active kinds of travelers. Confident, action-oriented, and adopting a no-frills mindset, they travel with purpose and intensity. They know exactly why they are traveling and are not easily dissuaded from their travel objectives.

(3) Transients
Persons just passing through a destination, perhaps on a brief stopover and only having a few hours, or a day, in a single location. Their limited time means that they have to be extremely strategic in their travel plans, visiting perhaps one or two major sites. They often travel alone and maximize their time by using taxis and staying in mainstream hotels.

(4) Backpackers
Often traveling in pairs and in their 20s, backpackers carry all their possessions on their back and tend to stay in hostels, hang out with other backpackers, have limited budgets, and are on the road for weeks or months at a time. They are a frequent sight at train stations, bus stops, and hostel lobbies. They are either returning from their last excursion or heading to their next destination. They may be on a gap year.

(5) Foodies
They are all about the next magical meal or inspiring beverage. Their budgets are connected to their culinary options. Street food, five-star dining, breweries, vineyards, cooking classes, and even meals at homes (these were always the best meals I had when in Cuba), culinary tourists plan an entire trip around their dining and beverage options. Group food tours include wine tastings, visits to local markets, eating at famous restaurants, and learning about the process of distillation or brewing. Such tours tend to cater to wealthier clientele.

(6) Nature Enthusiasts
They tend to stick to preserves, parks, zoos, and outdoor habitats. Birders, for instance, wear distinct clothing and may carry expensive photographic equipment. More amateur lovers of nature will spend the bulk of their time at national parks (such as volcanoes, waterfalls, and mountains), where they can hike, bike, swim, and ski to their hearts delight. Although they may visit popular landmarks, they prefer to be outdoors and usually do not stay in capitals or large cities for long, if at all.

(7) Adventurers
These are the guys and gals who just bungee jumped off a bridge toward a river filled with crocodiles or are traveling overseas to compete in some physical contest like a triathlon. Adventurers, sometimes called "thrill seekers," may visit Australia for surfing, Switzerland for hiking, Costa Rica for ziplining, or Zimbabwe for hunting. Adventurers bring their own supplies for camping or stay in eco-friendly establishments that tend to be in or close to nature.

(8) Partyers
Those who like to plan their trips around drinking, dancing, and having a good time have countless options available to them depending on their budget. Partyers come in all shades, stripes, and stages of life, but the quintessential party animals are spring breakers on holiday from college. They are a common fixture in festive destinations like Cancún, Mexico from February to April. They tend to stick with other party animals and are most active at night.

(9) Adult Learners
Many adults travel the world in order to learn and grow in their knowledge of other cultures. In reality, adult learners can represent any age group beyond high school, but many are professionals in their 50s, 60s, and 70s who may be retired

and have more time and money than most other travelers. Adult learners sometimes travel alone or in small groups, but they are often part of organized tours with specific objectives in mind.

(10) Students
These are some of the most common types of travelers. They may be part of a school or academic institution (and so part of a group of fellow students) or part of a study-abroad program, in which case they may be alone or in a small cohort. Students tend to be in their teens or twenties and so are distinguished from the adult learners previously mentioned. Much of their travel is organized by someone else.

(11) Missionaries
Those who travel for the purpose of spreading their faith are as old as travel itself. In general, there are two kinds: short-term and long-term missionaries. Most traveling overseas are short-term missionaries whose trips last anywhere from five to ten days. Short-term missionaries are active throughout the year, but they are commonly found overseas during school breaks and summer holidays. Short-term missionaries travel in groups, tend to work with agencies that organize all their food, transportation, and lodgings, and will dedicate a day a week to sightseeing and other cultural activities.

(12) Pilgrims
All world religions unite in their recognition that certain physical places—whether Jerusalem, Rome, Mecca, or Bodh Gaya—are especially charged with solemnity and worthy of veneration. Pilgrims, of all faiths and ethnicities, travel the world each year in search of the holy. Pilgrims stick with other fellow pilgrims and naturally lodge in places proximate to holy shrines, sacred temples, and religious sites. As Christians, there are many historically meaningful locations that serve as places of pilgrimage.

Figure 2.1 Millions Travel to Israel Every Year as Pilgrims.

(13) Honeymooners

They tend to stay in resorts and nice hotels and travel with tours organized by travel agents and hotels. Though they may veer out to famous sites or do outdoor activities, they will often return to their resorts and hotels in the evening. As expected, honeymooners tend to keep to themselves.

(14) Volunteers

Many people around the world give their free time and use their own resources as acts of service overseas. These are usually short-term volunteers who may work at orphanages, zoos, parks, retreat centers, non-governmental agencies, mission organizations, and many other institutions.

(15) Businesspersons

These are the women and men traveling for work. Because their primary reason for travel is job related, they are limited in their ability to sightsee, explore the region, and engage with local people other than those directly connected to their work. Not surprisingly, businesspersons tend to stay in airport hotels or in other locations in proximity to their job sites. They primarily use private transportation (rentals, Uber, and taxis) and eat either at their hotels or at establishments prescheduled with their clients or partners. Rather than hitting the town after a long day of meetings, they retire to their hotel rooms to catch up on emails or chat with their families back home.

So, Who Are You?

As you prepare for your trip, which kind of traveler will you be? And how do you think this will affect your trip? In this book, I will never sit in judgement of your travel mindset or motives. Your trip is your business. But there is one final item I would like to discuss. As you embark on your travels, I encourage you to consider embodying certain qualities that I have found to be make trips more enjoyable, enriching, and enduring.

Tourists versus Travelers: There Is a Difference

The language I use varies, but most people recognize a difference between "tourists" and "travelers." Speaking in generalities, "tourists" tend to isolate themselves and stay immersed within their own culture, clinging to it like a trusted blanket. They prefer their own food, they speak only their own language, and they avoid experiences that stretch or challenge them. They almost always stick to touristy establishments—whether restaurants, hotels, shops, or sites. For the most part, they are not motivated to process their thoughts and feelings in the form of journaling.

"Travelers," meanwhile, step outside of their comfort zones, display cultural humility, and attempt to interact more with the immediate community. They like to eat where locals eat, get off the beaten path, and make purchases that build the local economy. They are introspective, reflecting on their experiences and feelings. Even if they are following an itinerary, they are much more willing to take risks and improvise when an opportunity presents itself. Though by no means being confused for locals, travelers embody a more adventurous mindset. In a word, tourists tend to travel in a more insulated and passive way while travelers do so in a more vulnerable and active way.

As you think about who you want to be overseas, I challenge you to think more like a traveler than a tourist. This, by no means, suggests that you have to become someone you are not or abandon your reason for traveling. Regardless of your travel motives, for instance, there are ways that we can become more outwardly engaged, more self-aware, and more culturally adventurous. And to help make more concrete how this is possible, I list below six key characteristics of a traveler (in contrast to a tourist, who may embody only one or none of the characteristics).

6 Attributes of a Traveler

Teacher that I am, the attributes of a traveler are all listed in a convenient acronym that spells "travel": try, reflect, adapt, view, engage, and linger.

1. **Try:** Try something new almost every day. Going to the beach? Try surfing! Going to a Muslim country? Get a Turkish bath! Encounter some locals who look fun and kind? Invite them for dinner at their favorite restaurant! Every day, try something you have never done before.

2. **Reflect:** Reflect on your daily experiences and record them. Journaling is one of the most effective things you can do while traveling. I always encourage travelers to bring a journal and write something in it every single day. And be creative—a journal doesn't have to just be a narrative. You can draw pictures of something you saw, record phrases you heard that day, or just write down the emotions you are feeling.

3. **Adapt:** Recognize that you cannot control everything that you experience. Despite all the planning in the world, international travel always entails a certain level

of uncertainty and risk. Rather than get frazzled or lose your patience when something unplanned takes place, try to embrace it, and adapt as well as you can. Loosen up, let your hair down, and roll up your sleeves.

4. **View:** Choose to view the world from the perspective of the local culture. Whereas a tourist tends to only see things from his or her own point of a view, a traveler knows there are other ways to see the world.

5. **Engage:** Be an active traveler who is regularly engaging in conversation with local people and fellow travelers. Lean into your environment by asking questions, volunteering comments, and actively listening to those around you, especially local people shedding light on the region you are visiting.

6. **Linger:** Linger in the moment. Don't be too quick to rush off to the next site or move away from what could turn out to be an unplanned but life-changing encounter.

Figure 2.2 "Travelers" Try New Foods When Overseas. "Tourists" Do Not.

Conclusion

While preparing for your upcoming journey, consider adopting the mindset of a traveler over against that of a tourist. When you do so, you never know what kind of amazing opportunities may come your way. In my attempts to embody these attributes abroad, I have benefited in untold ways—receiving random invitations from locals to dine in their homes, attending amazing concerts and public events with people I just met, and much more besides. That's because when you branch out of the beaten path, play the part of a humble guest eager to learn, and start talking to people and graciously sharing your story, amazing things can happen.

Reflection Questions

1. What are your primary and secondary travel personas?

2. What type of traveler would be your polar opposite and why?

3. Why might it be advantageous to understand the mindset of other travelers?

4. What are two differences between a tourist and a traveler?

5. How could you apply the "travel" principles in everyday life?

CHAPTER 3
MONEY MATTERS

The Envelope System for Guatemala

When I was in graduate school, I was preparing for a trip to Antigua, Guatemala, a colonial city near the country's capital that is popular with travelers and a great place to experience Latin American culture. I did not have any money for the trip, so about a year beforehand I devised a strategy to pay for it by setting aside $20 in cash every time I took a shift as a waiter. Every night I came home from waiting tables, I pulled out $20, put it in an envelope from my safe labeled "Guatemala Fund," and went about my business. Although there were moments when I would have preferred to use that money for other things—such as going out to eat with friends, buying clothes, or using it to pay for school, I am thankful that I persevered. When the time finally arrived for me to purchase my ticket and depart for my trip, I was able to pay for everything in cash. By applying this simple strategy, removing all emotion from the equation, and sticking to a sound plan, I had an amazing experience in Guatemala without incurring any debt.

Getting Money *Before* Your Trip and Following a Budget *While* There

Traveling overseas is an expensive enterprise. Although there are great deals out there making it more affordable and attainable than in years past, it is still a luxury that not all can afford, even for those, ironically, going on mission trips or service projects. Depending on your destination, length, purpose, and class of travel, your international trip could cost thousands of dollars. And if you are traveling in order to study in a semester-abroad program, to volunteer long-term, or to pursue a gap year, it will cost considerably more. Additionally, once you arrive in-country, you now have the challenge of managing the money you have set aside in such a manner that you can cover all your expenses. This requires keen judgement, diligence, and self-control. In this chapter, I will divide our discussion about money matters into two parts: (i) figuring out how to obtain money for travel and (ii) learning how to apportion that money toward your expenses.

(I) OBTAINING MONEY FOR TRAVEL

This first section explores possible revenue streams for travel. I can say confidently that all of them work, but some are definitely better than others. The truth of the matter is that each of us comes to the travel table with unique resources, different earning potential, ongoing commitments, varying levels of debts, faith communities from a range of socio-economic backgrounds, and individual spending habits. Few of us are wealthy enough to simply withdraw the money from our bank account. As a result, we need to develop and then adopt a game plan that will put us on the road to success.

(1) Start a Travel Fund

If you love traveling and are in a financial position to do so, I highly recommend starting a travel fund. Years ago, for instance, I determined that I loved traveling and found it so meaningful that I wanted it to be a regular part of my life for as long as possible, regardless of the specific purpose for traveling: to vacation with my family, to serve others, or to learn more about a foreign culture. Therefore, it made perfect sense for me to open up a savings account dedicated exclusively to travel. This allows me to track my expenses much easier and always be certain exactly how much I have available when the travel urge strikes or when an opportunity emerges. When I started my travel fund, I searched for a bank that offered a savings account with the best perks. I wanted an account that would grow in interest each year and also provide a debit and credit card with excellent benefits for international travel. Years later, I still allocate a tenth of my income to this fund, and I never let it reach below a certain amount. I recognize we all have different priorities—particularly for me as a travel professional—but I find it easier to have my travel fund in its own bank account, separate from everything else, so that I am not tempted to draw funds from it to pay for regularly occurring monthly expenses.

Of course, if you are not in the position to open up a bank account for travel, or you work in a profession that uses cash, that is not a problem. Purchase a small safe (or a really durable cookie jar!) and use the envelope system that worked so well for my learning experience in Guatemala. It is the same principle—creating a fund for travel that is separate from your regular, ongoing expenses, and determining how much and how often you should contribute to it. Every once in a while, perhaps when you receive a bonus from work, a refund from a tax return, or a birthday check, squirrel it away into your travel account in order to boost your fund. You will be pleasantly surprised at how much you will have after a year or two of saving.

Pro Tip: Automation is the way to go to keep your mind on the prize and your emotions out of your decision making. Choose the percentage of your income that you want to allocate to your travel fund (for example, 5%), and set up a direct deposit to that account so you can go on autopilot and not worry where the money is going to come from to foot your travel bill or next mission trip.

(2) Reduce Your Expenses

I always reduce my expenses immediately before a trip and pivot that money into my travel fund. I find it is easier to decrease my spending right before a trip since I know I will be able to apply that money to something more satisfying, enjoyable, or charitable in just a matter of weeks. This can be accomplished in many ways. For instance, you could stop buying coffee at your favorite coffee shop several weeks before a trip. Or you could commit to cutting your entertainment bill for a few months. Determine how much money you spend every day on these habits and transfer the savings into your travel fund. There are lots of apps that enhance your ability to reduce expenses. Consider experimenting with Daily Budget or Budgt.

Pro Tip: Cancel your cable, gym, and streaming subscriptions for two months. For the same duration of time, do not go out to eat. Although this will be hard, this combination of cancellations could save you hundreds of dollars that you could use for travel. Besides, when you return home, you can always resume your subscriptions and head back to the gym or your favorite restaurant. They will all be happy to welcome you back. But, meanwhile, you would have been able to have a fabulous time overseas with the money you saved.

(3) Earn a Side Income

If we are honest with ourselves, many of us have the ability to earn extra money by doing something on the side. This could be achieved by waiting tables two nights a week, tutoring online, or driving for Uber or DoorDash. In fact, if you live alone or are traveling as a family, you might want to consider listing your house or apartment with Airbnb to rent while you are away. That extra income could cover the entirety of your lodging expenses, or at least part of your trip. Not able to do that? Then search for a seasonable job. Depending on the exact position you are seeking, there are jobs offered year-round that allow you to earn extra income without committing to anything long-term. All the extra money you make from this side hustle could be used for travel, whether as pocket money or for giving away to those in need when overseas. I have adopted this approach several times to help offset my travel expenses. You could, too. By the way, did you know that there are several apps that allow you to earn extra money? Check out BookScouter to sell your old books or try Ibotta or Receipt Hog to scan receipts from your everyday purchases and receive rebates in return.

Pro Tip: Make a list of 10 ways you could earn additional income based on your interests, skills, background, education, and locale. Were you a waiter during high school? Then write "waiting tables" as a possibility. Did you play a sport in college? Then put "coach" down as an option. Now, shave that list from 10 to 5. After doing research and exploring the possibilities, cut that number to 2 and then pick the job that offers the most earning potential or has the most flexibility. It's easier than you think.

(4) Raise Funds or Find a Sponsor

If you are in high school or college, fundraising or seeking a sponsorship is a common way to pay for international travel. In fact, this is also standard for church trips, volunteering abroad, sports travel, and educational opportunities. Historically, for instance, groups going on mission trips raise funds by washing cars, selling sweets, creating raffles, holding auctions, hosting luncheons, putting on yard sales, and doing yard work for donations. This old-style approach can still work depending on the context, so do not immediately dismiss it. In today's technological age, however, it is increasingly popular to fundraise or seek a sponsor through online platforms, which are free to use and able to generate a lot of money from a variety of donors. I have had a lot of travelers earn all of their funds by using these platforms. Or, if you want to get creative and design a product to earn funds related to your travel—like clothes, an app, some innovative service, or some other contraption—then check out Indiegogo or Crowdfunder. These are solid platforms that give you access to millions of potential donors.

Pro Tip: Crowdfunding is the way to go to secure funds for travel if you are looking for the largest pool of possible donors and sponsors. Simply visit one of the sites I mentioned, such as GoFundMe or Fundly, and begin bringing awareness to your cause. Upload compelling pictures, speak to the heart, be succinct, set a target goal, and make your case.

(5) Sell Something You Own

If you are like most people, you own clothes you no longer wear, keep trinkets you no longer want, and possess electronics you no longer use. This could be anything—jewelry, baseball cards, golf clubs, cell phones, you name it. Fortunately, you can put these items to good use. Search through your belongings and ask yourself if you would rather continue owning that brand-new tennis racket collecting dust in your shed or apply the money you could make from selling it to take an underground tour of the catacombs in Rome. I speak from experience when I say that the memory you make walking through the cobwebs where ancient Christians buried their dead outvalues the cobwebs forming on your racket.

Pro Tip: Open up an eBay or Craigslist account and start rummaging through your garage, basement, or attic for things you no longer use, want, or need. Sell them online or do a yard sale. Apply all the proceeds to your travel fund.

Figure 3.1 Before You Go Overseas, Have a
Yard Sale to Earn Some Extra Cash.

Before You Go Overseas

(6) Search for a Grant
Believe it or not, the only thing separating you from traveling the world for free is finding a grant for which you qualify. Unfortunately, this is easier said than done. Unlike loans that require repayment plus interest, grants and scholarships are money you receive but do not have to pay back. There are countless grants and scholarships available, but it takes patience and diligence to locate them, qualify for them, apply to them, and obtain them. I have received several over my career. Most recently, I obtained a grant that allowed me to study in England, and another one that covered all my expenses to do research in Germany for an entire summer. These grants are not growing on trees, but they do exist, so go hunting for any such low-hanging fruit. Most grants are funded by a specific industry, school, foundation, corporation, denomination, or agency, so you will have to look in a variety of places to locate one that fits your interests and background. Get started with GoAbroad, Partners, and GrantWatch.

Pro Tip: If you want to see the world and serve others by teaching, consider teaching English as a Second Language. You can get paid to teach and mentor students as well as find time to travel. Keep in mind, though, that not all agencies are created equal. Find one that is reputable and has good reviews and realize what you are signing up for before signing a contract.

(7) Apply for a Student Loan
Common financial wisdom says that you should only take loans for items that appreciate over time or generate future earning power, such as a house or a college education. This is sound advice, and my preference is to never incur debt for travel. That said, it does make sense in some specific situations. For instance, students who are studying overseas for a semester or year will likely only be able to do so by taking out student loans. This is how most of my groups from colleges and universities finance their travel. If you need to borrow money as a student in order

to travel, do so wisely, searching for the lowest interest rates and best repayment plans, from a firm with a solid history and reputation, never requesting more than needed so that you can keep your debt within reach. Having a budget firmly in place is essential for this option.

Pro Tip: At your college or school, set up an appointment with the financial aid office and explain your situation. Search for a loan that offers the lowest interest rate or most flexible payback schedule. Choose a provider that you can trust.

(8) Put It on Your Credit Card?

I have a friend who funded her own six-month volunteer training program by paying for it on her credit card. At the time, she had no job, no savings, and she earned no income for volunteering. When I asked her how she intended to pay the bill, she said, "Oh, I'll just work half a day a week somewhere and pay the minimum bill on my credit card." Although she meant well, this is not a good approach to paying for travel. The interest rates on credit cards are scandalously high, which means that you could end up paying dearly for your trip months and even years afterward. For instance, the average interest rate for a credit card is 17%. This adds up quickly. A much better approach is saving your money over the course of a year or two or earning side income and then setting that money aside in a travel fund that you can then use to cover your trip.

Pro Tip: I have already registered my caution against this approach, but, if you need to pay for travel with a credit card that you do not immediately intend to pay in full, then at least apply for a credit card that will give you a trial period with no interest and with the lowest amount of interest after the promotion ends. Then use this new credit card to purchase your trip. It goes without saying that you will want to pay the amount back as quickly as possible in order to reduce the interest owed. Always know your interest rate.

(II) BUDGETING FOR TRAVEL

Now that we have created a pathway toward earning the funds needed for travel, we have to learn how to astutely allocate those funds toward our actual expenses. You can do this the old-fashioned way—with pen and paper—or you can do this on your computer by using a Word or Excel document. Even better, there are dozens of apps available that can help you build a budget from scratch with the click of a button on your smart phone. Whatever approach you take—on paper, with a computer, or on your phone—this step must be taken at an early stage in your travel plans. Although your budget does not have to be precise, it does need to be as accurate as possible. Traveling to Israel, for instance, is much more expensive than neighboring Lebanon, just as visiting Costa Rica will cost much more than its neighbor Nicaragua. These realities cannot be overlooked unless you want to be severely disappointed. Fortunately, there are many ways to find this information. If you are traveling on your own, the internet will be your best gauge for prices. But if you are part of a group tour, your budgeting is uncomplicated: You pay the price advertised and simply ask the agency, church, or school about any excluded costs, such as trip insurance and other miscellaneous expenses.

(1) Determine Your Budget

How much money are you able to spend on your trip? If you are part of a group tour, the costs are fixed and already determined by the overseeing agency. However, if you are traveling alone or with a small crew, then you get to decide how much you will set aside for your trip. There is no silver bullet to determining your costs. It is a deeply personal decision. Perhaps you go overseas three times a year, in which case you will need a tighter budget. Or perhaps you have never traveled abroad before and it is your 50th birthday, in which case there is just cause for splurging. Each of these factors into your budget. Speaking in generalities,

I think anywhere from 5% to 10% of your annual income is not unreasonable to spend overseas, especially given that you are financially responsible.

Of course, if you follow my advice above about creating a travel fund, then you will need to stay within the amount of money located in that account. One last consideration is the actual cost of the trip you want to take. You may have an idea that your group tour to Greece only costs $3,500, but after following the steps below you may realize that it actually costs double that amount. If so, you may have to alter your plans, deciding (a) how long it will take to afford this tour or (b) whether you can lower the price by shortening your stay, staying in cheaper hotels, or applying airline miles.

Pro Tip: If you are uncertain as to how much you should set aside for an international trip and you do not yet have a travel fund that limits your spending, then simply let your net monthly income be your yearly travel amount. This makes things remarkably straightforward: Just find last month's payment stub and let that number be the maximum amount for your trip. For a book to help you stay on top of your budget when traveling, consider Matt Kepnes, *How to Travel the World on $50 a Day* (New York: Penguin, 2015).

(2) Allocate Your Expenses

After deciding your budget, you will now need to apply that money toward all of your travel expenses. The exact percentages per allocation will vary according to multiple factors, such as destination, time of year, airline cabin preference, and level of hotel, but I have ranked the following from most expensive to least expensive under most circumstances. If you want to search for prices based on a specific country, go to BudgetYourTrip.com. This site will help you determine more accurate expenses per region. When searching for prices, write down approximate amounts for each of these categories. In the next section, we will discuss where to find the costs for each of these allocations.

Before You Go Overseas

- Airfare
- Lodging
- Meals
- Tours/Excursions/Guides
- Ground Transportation
- Passport/Visa
- Medical/Vaccinations
- Entertainment
- Insurance
- Trip Gear/Clothes
- Tips/Gifts
- Snacks
- Souvenirs
- Exit/Entry Country Fees
- Foreign Transaction Fees
- Miscellaneous

Pro Tip: It's easy to overlook foreign transaction fees and exchange rates when allocating your expenses. However, these fees and rates add up quickly when overseas. Apply for a credit card with zero foreign transaction fees and only use debit cards in-country to withdraw cash so you can keep down exchange rates.

(3) Research All Your Allocated Costs
Your next step is to price out each of the categories listed above. You have at your disposal three main sources of information for doing so: (i) travel guidebooks, (ii) the internet, and (iii) friends or family familiar with your destination. When I prepare for a trip, I consult each of these sources in this order, which I classify as (i) experts, (ii) amateurs, and (iii) tourists. All three loops of feedback are helpful since they emanate from different perspectives.

I begin budgeting with guidebooks, which are written by expert travelers who know the terrain like the back of their hands. There are lots of publishers and authors out there, so consult as many as possible in order to determine which one you like best. For instance, Rick Steves is a definite go-to if you are budgeting for a trip to Europe. He conducts meticulous research and tells you exactly how much everything costs. But Lonely Planet, Rough Guides, and Fodor's are also known brands that have stood the test of time. Before you buy a guidebook, consider visiting your local library or bookstore to see which books are available and which ones you like most. Guidebooks should be able to provide you with up-to-date prices on lodging, food, tours, excursions, transportation, entertainment, as well as exit and entry country fees. List all these expenses in your budget.

Next, begin scouring the internet for budget tips related to your destination. Check out blogs, travel websites, and YouTube. Here, your success will be hit-or-miss. Some websites are exceptional, written by people who love traveling and have an eye for detail, dishing out excellent travel tips and offering inside scoops on how to budget for your destination. Others are click-bait that offer nothing of value. Lastly, try to reach out to a friend or family member who may have experience traveling to the place(s) you want to visit. Listen to what they have to say.

It's possible you will have to bypass this last step, and that is not a problem. The primary sources of information for budgeting will come from guidebooks and the internet. When budgeting for airfare, go online to Expedia, Kayak, Google Flights, or directly to your preferred airline for that information. Don't forget to browse the web incognito, which will allow you to get the best rates every time you search.

Pro Tip: In addition to guidebooks, you will need to become familiar with apps and popular websites like Expedia, Viator, Triposo, Kayak, Hotels.com, Airbnb, Rome2Rio, and TripAdvisor. When it comes to budgeting, these will give you a ball-park figure about how much everything is going to cost. Whether air, lodging, transportation, food, museums, or entertainment, these apps and sites have you covered, and they will become trusted guides when traveling. Although you do not have to make any purchases through them, I still recommend using them to build an accurate budget for all your travel expenses.

(4) Add Your Expenses
Now that you have uncovered all your costs, you are ready to add your expenses. All you need to do is combine everything from your budgeting chart into one sum. As before, you can do this (i) with pen and paper, (ii) in a computer document or spreadsheet, or (iii) on your cell phone. There is nothing too difficult about this step. It is simply calculating all of your estimates, so that you can have an accurate figure from which to work. If you think the figure is too high, then you may need to reduce your number of nights, cut your entertainment budget, or travel during off-season. But if the figure is attainable, then all you have left to do is to simply keep track of all your expenses once you arrive.

    Pro Tip: Consider using Goodbudget. It is a software program based on the envelope system, which is great when it comes to categorizing multiple expenses. It will allow you to instantly allocate your costs toward specific spending categories.

(5) Track Your Expenses
Your final step toward successfully allocating your resources is simply keeping track of everything. On previous trips, I used to bring a small notebook to record all my expenses by hand. Because my days are usually terribly busy, I did this late at night or early in the morning. This sufficed, but it was labor-intensive. Nowadays, I can do all of the work with my cell phone. I can simply take pictures of my receipts and an app will do the math and keep me updated about how much money I have left. There are many apps that can help track and monitor your expenses.

Consider YouNeedABudget (YNAB), TripCoin, TrailWallet, TravelSpend, and PocketGuard.

Pro Tip: If you want an all-in-one finance app, check out Mint. It is a great tool to use. It instantly tracks your expenses and can send alerts when you go off track. Because it is a comprehensive money management platform, it can be used for far more than just travel.

Conclusion

Finding and managing money is one of the most stressful and time-consuming of all travel endeavors. For some, it is their biggest hurdle. Fortunately, though, it is now easier than ever to earn money for travel as well as allocate it responsibly once you have it. Today, there are countless websites and apps that streamline and simplify this entire process, meaning that you can spend your time on more exciting prospects, like daydreaming about your itinerary and anticipating all you will see, do, and explore while overseas.

Reflection Questions

1. Which funding options appealed to you most? Was there one you will not use?

2. Are there any side hustles you do or could do that would pay for your traveling expenses?

3. What is your preferred method of keeping track of money: pen and paper, computer, or smart phone?

4. If you realized you lacked the finances for an educational trip, would you cut the length of your trip, postpone it until you have adequate funds, stay at cheaper hotels, or go into debt?

5. Is there anyone you know who has traveled overseas that would help in allocating a budget?

CHAPTER 4
LOGISTICS COORDINATION

Thank You, Singapore

I remember the very first time I had to manage logistics for a large group completely on my own with no assistance. I was traveling to Singapore and was so thankful for the incredibly user-friendly infrastructure the region provided: efficient transportation, food galore—the single best food, in fact, of any place I have ever visited—excellent accommodations in a variety of different neighborhoods, paved and connected roads, a safe and secure society, and endless activities. But an easy-to-navigate infrastructure is not always offered when traveling abroad. And when it's not, it's essential to have time-tested assistance that you can trust.

Is It Really Possible to Manage Logistics?

Logistics. The very word strikes fear in the heart of countless travelers. With so many details to manage—some requiring extreme minutiae and others large quantities of time and patience—it's little wonder that so many travelers delay their plans until the last minute, fail to complete them altogether, or place the burden on someone else.

Logistics, however, doesn't have to be difficult. I have successfully arranged logistics for trips across the world, each carrying their own degree of challenges, but none of them impossible nor out of reach for anyone committed to following a sensible series of steps. What's more, with the constant arrival of so many excellent apps at your fingertips (below, I include at least two apps per step), international travel is easier to arrange than ever before. Today, with the press of a button, you can build your itinerary, buy your flight, select your insurance, arrange your accommodations, track your expenses, and secure your transportation. It's a great time to be alive.

10 Chronological Steps

Though not essential, I recommend following each step in the order listed. And keep in mind that each one should be followed *before* stepping foot on a plane. If you are using a travel agent, your job just got a lot easier. A travel agent can accomplish several of these steps in his or her sleep, which means that you don't have to lose any while you wait for the tasks to be completed.

Travel agents and providers are definitely valuable and important players in the tourism industry, and it goes without saying that one or both is needed for large group trips, but for those who travel alone or in small groups, they are not necessary. Below, I am assuming that you will organize most of the trip details yourself, so there is limited discussion about the pros and cons of travel agents and providers. But even if you are not planning everything on your own—and someone else is arranging these details for you—it is still important to review the steps in order to become familiar with what is needed for international travel and to ensure that your agent or provider doesn't miss any details.

(1) Itinerary

Your itinerary is your architectural blueprint. It precedes everything else. It casts a vision for your trip, details the destinations you will visit, limits your number of days, calculates your costs, establishes contingency plans, and explains how you will get from place to place. Even if you prefer to keep your options open when traveling, you still need a rough outline so that you can secure your travel dates and estimate your expenses. Stated differently, this is the step where you actively plan your budget. If you are looking for traditional sites and activities for your itinerary, I recommend the apps VisitACity and Viator. You may also want to consider Triposo, which will allow you to personalize your travel plans.

Pro Tip: Make a contingency plan for each day of your trip *before* going overseas. Better to research and determine all your options when calm and collected than when a group of disappointed and impatient travelers is staring you down in a foreign country (I speak from experience).

(2) Passport

Gone are the days when you could use your Driver's License to travel internationally. If you want to see the world, you need a passport. Also, neither the airline nor the country you are visiting will admit you if your passport expires within 6 months of entry. For adults in the US, a valid passport lasts 10 years. Be sure to keep yours current. You may also want to consider downloading the app MobilePassport, which can save you time at the airport when returning home. Also, as I discuss elsewhere, make two copies of your passport. Keep the first at home in a safe or filing cabinet but take the second with you (keeping it secure yet in a separate place from your actual passport in case one is lost).

Pro Tip: Never pay more for your passport than necessary. Renew it when it gets within a year of expiration so that you do not pay an expedited rate. If you think you will forget to renew your passport on time, use the app RushMyPassport.

(3) Flights

Each airline manages its own policies regarding how far in advance you can book tickets, but it is usually no more than 11 months. When is the best time to secure your tickets? It depends on many factors—number of travelers, destination, budget, cabin preference, airline carrier, layover options, etc. In general, if you are part of a group and want to fly together, then booking tickets to 8 to 10 months in advance is ideal. If you like to live on the edge, that is fine, but I still recommend you secure your ticket *at least* 2 months in advance—if for no other reason that there are other required steps when preparing for travel, particularly the next step, which is time-sensitive. The app Hopper says that it can predict the best time to purchase a ticket with 95% accuracy. Check it out next time you are searching for flights. Kayak is another popular app that provides you with the best rates.

Pro Tip: Several airline carriers let you to spend a night (or more) in one of their hubs at no additional cost. This allows you to visit a whole other country in addition to your primary destination.

(4) Visa

Every country is different—and if you are a US Citizen, you are able to visit dozens of destinations without a Visa—but some nations still require a Visa to enter. Sometimes these Visas can be purchased when you arrive in-country; other times, you must have a valid Visa beforehand, or you will be denied entry. And one more thing: You cannot obtain your Visa until *after* you have a booked flight, which is why securing your flight must precede applying for a Visa. I always thought it counter-productive to do it in this order. What happens, for instance, if you purchase a ticket but are denied a Visa? Yet, this is the way it works. Flights, then Visa. In terms of apps, consider TravelVisa, VisaHQ, or iVisa.

Pro Tip: If the country you are visiting sells both pre-country and in-country Visas, purchase your Visa in advance. It will be cheaper.

(5) Accommodations

Depending on where you are going, accommodations can fill up quickly. When I take groups to Israel, for instance, I need to secure accommodations nine months in advance in order to guarantee the best lodging at the best rates. If you are traveling alone or are part of a small group and are flexible, however, you could wait 1 to 3 months before arranging your lodging. Two of my go-to apps for accommodations, among many others, are Airbnb and Hotels.com.

Pro Tip: Never book your lodging without (a) viewing its location on Google Maps and (b) reading at least 25 reviews. Accommodations make or break a trip.

Figure 4.1 Where You Stay Is Crucial. Read at
Least 25 Reviews Before Booking a Place.

(6) Insurance

By this time, you know the cost of your trip and have booked all of the essentials. Now is the time to purchase travel insurance. I devote the next chapter entirely to this topic. To summarize, I recommend contacting three providers and choosing the best rate offered, even if you just choose the most basic policy. Three popular providers are Allianz, Generali, and International SOS.

Pro Tip: If you want the most comprehensive coverage—called Cancel for Any Reason (CAFR) insurance—then you should purchase it within 24 hours of making your initial trip payment.

(7) Transportation

Do not wait until you arrive in-country before determining how you will get to your hotel, or how you will get from your hotel to the places you plan to visit. Not only is this more expensive in the long run, but it also causes more stress and longer wait times. And don't think that you can always order an Uber in-country. As popular as this company is, there are still many countries and towns where it is unavailable or restricted by law. Research and secure your transportation before going overseas—whether booking a rental car, purchasing a train ticket ahead of time, scheduling an Uber or Lyft pickup, or researching the timetable of the public bus system. Expedia and Rome2Rio are apps that I frequently use for arranging transportation, and I prefer Waze when driving overseas.

Pro Tip: Public transportation is always cheaper than a taxi, Uber, or a professional transportation company. Most international airports offer safe, reliable, and inexpensive transport to the most popular destinations at a fraction of the cost of private transport. Check out the website of the airport you are flying into for rates and reservations.

(8) Meals

There is nothing like wandering the streets of your new destination and choosing the restaurant or street vendor that smells and looks the best. When I go to places like Singapore and Istanbul and Paris, for instance, I like to keep my culinary options open. However, this style of travel does not work for large groups. With groups of ten or more, you need to arrange most of your meals beforehand. One of my favorite apps for researching restaurants is TripAdvisor, which contains reviews, prices, addresses, and even menu items for restaurants around the world; see also the app TheFork, which is a subsidiary of TripAdvisor. For annotating your food expenses, consider the app TrabeePocket.

Pro Tip: For big groups, I arrange breakfast and dinner to be eaten each day at a hotel. This not only makes the most of our time, but it also can be purchased at a discount and put easily on one bill or added to a room number.

(9) Reconfirmation

Customs vary greatly from one country to another. When I was once flying out of Cuzco, Peru, for instance, I was bumped from my fully purchased flight because I had not previously "confirmed" it. I complained to the attendant that my purchase of the ticket was my "confirmation" that I intended to fly, but it did not matter. Years later, in Riga, Latvia, I experienced the same thing. Long story short: You need to reconfirm ALL your reservations one to three weeks before your departure: flight, lodging, transportation, major meals, etc. Better to appear overzealous than arrive at an airport or hotel only to realize you booked the wrong dates or a clerical oversight had overlooked or deleted your reservation.

Pro Tip: Send your email travel confirmations to the app TripIt, which will organize all your travel plans into one convenient place.

(10) Money

The last step in your logistics planning is securing the cash you will need overseas. (The former chapter is devoted exclusively to money matters, particularly where you get money for travel and how to budget it accordingly.) Note that you should have already estimated your expenses for the trip in the first step: making an itinerary. As such, all you are doing now is (a) contacting your credit card and debit card companies to notify them of your travel plans and (b) withdrawing some cash from your ATM. (Never travel to a country without some cash.) I like to use the app TripCoin for keeping track of my money when abroad, and XECurrency comes in handy when factoring in exchange rates. The app TrailWallet is also popular for expense tracking.

Pro Tip: Withdraw a small amount of local currency from an ATM machine at the airport upon arrival. Only do so with a debit card (never a credit card, which usually charges exorbitant transaction fees). Remember: Debit cards are for withdrawing cash while credit cards (preferably with no foreign transaction fees) are for making purchases. At the same time, always keep some spare change in the local currency for tips, snacks, or bathrooms (yes, many countries around the world charge for their bathrooms).

Conclusion

Upon following these 10 simple steps, you will be arranging logistics like an expert travel agent. But even if you are using a professional planner to arrange some travel details, it is still recommended to review the steps. Although coordinating travel plans can be stressful, do not forget to revel in the anticipation of traveling to an exciting destination. Or, if you are not traveling overseas yourself, know that your hard work is going to make travel for someone else so much smoother and so much more enjoyable. Every bit of planning in the beginning pays off in the end.

Reflection Questions

1. Are you the person who normally plans a trip or do you ask someone else to do that?

2. Depending on your answer above, how much responsibility would you give a travel agent?

3. Are you familiar with any of these apps? Which interest you the most?

4. What kind of travel insurance would you likely pick? Have you known people burned by choosing ill-fitting insurance?

5. How closely does your travel preparation mirror the ten steps listed? Did you notice time frames associated with each step?

CHAPTER 5
TRAVEL INSURANCE

Kenya On Hold

I was preparing a group for an international trip scheduled for Kenya. We had already booked airline tickets, arranged accommodations and transportation, and were ready for what promised to be an exhilarating experience. But the trip never occurred. Just a couple of weeks before departing, a series of terrorist attacks had destabilized the city in which we were going to stay, and our safety could no longer be guaranteed. Unfortunately, we had to cancel our trip, but I was never more thankful to have trip insurance. We were able to salvage most all of our investment, whereas we would have lost most all of it had we not purchased the insurance plan offering maximum coverage.

Travel Insurance

Despite our best intentions, travel schedules can sometimes change, face interruptions, or encounter delays due to natural disasters, sudden illness, disease outbreak, family emergency, terrorism, or some other unforeseen reason. When the unpredictable occurs, travel insurance can help minimize your loss.

Recommended

I highly encourage travelers to purchase insurance for their trips and flights. There are countless providers available, and there are just as many kinds of plans. Please note that Thomas Institute does not provide or sell insurance or cover losses due to travel interruption. The best way to protect your trip is to purchase insurance.

Figure 5.1 I Recommend Every Traveler Purchase Travel Insurance.

Cancel for Any Reason (CAFR)—The Most Comprehensive Plan Available

The most comprehensive, and expensive, package is what is commonly referred to as "Cancel for Any Reason" (CAFR) insurance. It usually costs several hundred dollars per person, and most policies only reimburse up to 75% of your trip. In general, this policy must be purchased within one day to two weeks of making your initial payment (the exact time depends on the provider, but you have to act very quickly for CAFR insurance to be available). With all the fears of the Coronavirus (COVID-19) that began in 2020, CAFR insurance was essentially the only kind of insurance available that could definitively protect trip costs from the virus. There are other eligibility requirements for CAFR insurance, however, so you will need to familiarize yourself with those before purchasing it.

Kinds of Insurance Plans

Less comprehensive insurance policies cover a range of items—anything from trip delay to health issues to loss of baggage. These policies can be much cheaper, but they offer limited coverage.

In general, there are four major kinds of insurance plans:
- Trip cancellation and interruption
- Flight insurance
- Baggage loss
- Medical and health

There are also plans covering evacuation, theft, automobiles, and other items. In short, if you can think of something disastrous that could happen while traveling, insurance companies have found a way to anticipate it and provide protective measures—the more money you spend, the more protections you receive.

You May Already Have Existing Coverage

You may also want to check with your credit card or existing insurance provider for home, medical, car, or life coverage to see whether you may already be protected when you travel.

Each of these policies contains a highly detailed list of inclusions and exclusions. Travel Guard, for instance, contains plans organized into "Deluxe," "Preferred," and "Essential," each with varying degrees of coverage. Similarly, Generali Global Assistance arranges its plans into "Standard," "Preferred," and "Premium." As mentioned above, the more coverage you choose, the higher the cost.

Of course, some people just want the basics, and these are usually the cheapest plans available, perhaps as little as 5% of your total trip cost. But every person and trip is unique, and it carries different degrees of risk, so it is recommended to talk with an agent online, through email, or over the phone to find the plan that best serves your needs.

Consider Your Concerns before Speaking with an Agent

Before you contact a provider, I suggest you jot down all your travel fears and concerns. Are you worried about being able to return home quickly if a loved one is in need? Are you afraid that your luggage could get lost or stolen? Or are you more concerned about an existing medical condition that could flare up while overseas? Once your concerns are on paper and thoroughly processed, you will have a better idea of what kind of policy to purchase.

Best Time to Purchase Insurance

When is the best time to purchase insurance? Right away! **I recommend purchasing travel insurance within 24 hours of making your deposit or initial payment.** This will offer you the best possible rates and access to the most comprehensive coverage. The longer you wait, the higher the quote you may receive or the less comprehensive the coverage you may be eligible for. And it goes without saying that you cannot purchase insurance retroactively—insurance only works if you purchase it *before* an incident occurs. However, basic coverage is available up until the day before your trip.

You will, of course, want to read all the fine print before purchasing a plan. There is nothing worse than spending money on insurance only to find out that your specific incident is not covered.

Cost of Insurance Plans

How much does insurance cost? The only way to determine an exact price is to contact an insurance company and provide them with specific details about yourself and your trip. Policies can vary greatly depending on age, state of residence, medical history, and cost of trip. However, the average amount is somewhere between 4% to 12% of your total trip cost.

What kind of questions will the insurance company ask you? In general, they will want to ascertain the following:

- Nationality and state of residence
- Age
- Number of travelers
- Total cost of trip
- Dates of trip
- Country/countries visiting
- Existing medical conditions
- Kinds of coverage you are seeking

Once the travel company receives this information, they will provide you with a specific quote. Keep in mind that a quote only lasts for a certain period of time, and your coverage is not activated *until* you purchase the plan and receive confirmation—usually in an email that contains the terms of the coverage you purchased. I personally like to request quotes from three different companies in order to guarantee the best possible rate.

Common Providers

Here are some well-known insurance providers, most all of which I have used in the past on different occasions:

- Travelex
- Travel Guard
- Allianz Travel
- Travel Safe
- Travel Insurance

- Insure My Trip
- International SOS
- Generali Global Assistance

Conclusion

To summarize, I highly recommend that you purchase travel insurance. The decision is up to you, of course, and you should do whatever is most comfortable and makes the most sense for your particular needs and concerns. As you consider your insurance options, here is a summary of the steps to follow:

1. Write down your greatest travel concerns and fears.

2. Contact three different providers online. Provide each with information about yourself and your trip and request a quote.

3. Compare and contrast each policy to ensure it covers what you want.

4. Purchase the policy that is best for you and keep a copy of it available when traveling.

5. If you experience an incident while traveling (that is covered by your policy), you will mostly likely have to pay all the costs up-front while in-country. Then you will need to file an insurance claim; if approved, which can take days or weeks, the insurance company will reimburse you.

To be sure, no one wants to think about how an eagerly anticipated trip can go wrong, but the best way to allay any concerns you might have about travel interruptions, changes, injuries, or cancellations is to purchase the policy that is best for you. As the saying goes, "better safe than sorry."

Before You Go Overseas

Reflection Questions

1. Everybody has a story where their travel plans went awry. Which one do you remember most vividly?

2. Off the top of your head, which travel insurance fits you the best?

3. When is the best time to purchase travel insurance?

4. How can you guarantee the best possible rate on a travel quote?

5. Reading the fine print can be a hassle, but it safeguards against surprises. Have you even been surprised when coverage wasn't what you expected?

CHAPTER 6
RISK MANAGEMENT

Managing in Morocco

We were traveling to Morocco, definitely one of the most exciting destinations of the world. However, our visit occurred almost immediately after 9/11, and we were warned that American travelers could face possible risks given the global tension, especially in a Muslim-majority country. We took the warnings with the utmost seriousness and considered canceling our plans. However, we ultimately decided to continue with our trip as scheduled. Fortunately, everything turned out better than anticipated, but we had several plans in place that mitigated and avoided any risks we thought we might possibly encounter.

Risk Is Unavoidable but Manageable

Life is all about managing risk. Should I invest my savings in the stock market or keep it in the bank? Should I rent an apartment or buy a home? Should I become a teacher or an architect? Should I take my bike to work or order an Uber? Every day, we are bombarded with big and small decisions alike—all of which carry some level of risk. Naturally, some decisions are riskier than others, but none of us can escape a life without risk. After all, managing risk is part of being human, and it is especially part of being a traveler in the twenty-first century.

Defining and Classifying Risk

What exactly is a risk? Generally speaking, a risk is an uncertain event or outcome that, if it occurs, produces a negative effect. Of course, a risk can also turn out positively, but we will focus our discussion below on the negative effects of risk.

All individuals and organizations respond to risk in their own way. According to *A Guide to the Project Management Body of Knowledge*, risk is organized into three types: (a) *risk appetite*, (b) *risk tolerance*, and (c) *risk threshold*. Briefly defined, risk appetite is the degree of uncertainty a person is willing to assume in anticipation of a reward; risk tolerance is the amount of risk a person can withstand; and risk threshold is the standard by which accepting or avoiding risk is measured. I recommend that you take time thinking about these definitions and determining where you stand in relation to them. And at the end of our discussion, I will list the four major ways that people and groups respond to risk.

RISK: Research, Identify, Safeguard, Keep

As you consider the risks involved in international travel, I advise the following steps—arranged in the acronym RISK—which stands for **R**esearch, **I**dentify, **S**afeguard, and **K**eep. Altogether, these verbs take into consideration country-specific risks, likelihood and impact of risks, financial risks, and safety risks.

(1) Country-Specific Risks: Research the places you will visit.

Every location in the world carries with it a unique and country-specific degree of risk. Some, for instance, will require visiting a travel clinic to ensure that you are up-to-date on all your vaccinations, while others will require no additional medical treatment. Similarly, some countries score very high on the Corruption Perceptions Index (or CPI), while others score very low. As you research your destination, you will quickly learn how to prepare for a safe and secure trip.

One of the best sources of information is the U.S. Department of State's Bureau of Consular Affairs. The "International Travel" section of this website collects excellent data about each global destination, including health and safety concerns.

Be sure to familiarize yourself with your destination by reading the Department of State's profile in full. Check for any Travel Advisories.

Under the DOS Travel Advisory system, each country is assigned a specific color and number: (1) Level 1 - Exercise Normal Precautions; (2) Level 2 - Exercise Increased Caution; (3) Level 3 - Reconsider Travel; and (4) Level 4 - Do Not Travel. It is recommended not to visit any countries with a Level 3 or 4. You may also want to review the CIA World Factbook for each country you will be visiting.

Be sure to learn about each country's specific laws, customs, language, currency, and social norms. Learn basic phrases in the language spoken, become familiar with the major religion practiced, take note of any unusual laws or customs, and write down the country's currency and exchange rates. (I like to make a sheet the size of a credit card that has easy conversions for $1, $5, $10, $20, $50, and $100, which I can quickly consult when making purchases, or file it in my notes on my smartphone.)

(2) Likelihood and Impact of Risks: Identify (and begin mitigating) the most immediate risks.

After you have done the necessary research, you are ready to additionally identify any health, economic, or security risks. For example, if exploring the Amazon Rainforest, mitigate your health risks by taking malaria pills, using mosquito repellent, wearing long-sleeves and pants, and recording the address of the nearest health clinic. If visiting Iraq, mitigate your safety risks by registering your trip with the Department of State (in the Smart Traveler Enrollment Program), avoiding neighborhoods known for violence, and locating the nearest police department or US Consulate or Embassy. And if traveling to a large city like Paris, mitigate your economic risks by carrying a "dummy wallet" (with just a few dollars in it, so that it satisfies a pick pocketer or mugger) and by keeping aware of your surroundings and tourist scams.

How do you determine which risks are most urgent or immediate? I recommend screening all possible risks through a likelihood and impact filter. For each possible risk, ask two related questions: Is this risk *likely* to occur? And what will its *impact* be? When considering risks, I chart them out based on a scale of 1 to 10. If a risk carries high likelihood and high impact, you need to have a mitigation plan B firmly in place and take aggressive and proactive action. Conversely, if it carries low likelihood and low impact, then it requires little attention. Because time is always one of the most limited resources you have, you will need to prioritize all risks according to a likelihood and impact chart so that you address only what really needs to be addressed—and in the order of importance.

In addition to identifying and begin mitigating against the most immediate risks, also consider lessening your risks in-country by deciding beforehand how you will secure: (a) insurance, (b) an emergency plan, (c) transportation, (d) accommodations, and (e) food. (These topics are discussed in more depth in the chapter on logistics coordination.) And be sure to remember that, among college-age travelers, motor-vehicle accidents are the leading cause of death. Always exercise extreme caution when crossing streets, using the subway or public bus, or when driving in a foreign country.

(3) Financial Risks: Safeguard your valuables.

While traveling overseas, you will always need to keep your passport, money, phone, computer, and other valuables in a safe location (and keep a <u>copy</u> of your passport in a separate place). I personally recommend placing your passport, most cash, an extra credit card, and other valuables in a locked safe. If that is not possible, keep your valuables in a money belt around your waste (preferably tucked under your shirt or pants) or in some other place that makes it difficult for a thief to locate.

When withdrawing money from a bank or ATM, do so discreetly and pocket your cash before exiting. Do not draw attention to yourself, and do not carry or count money openly in view of others. Be sure to keep safe whatever is of greatest value to you—whether medicine, money, or some other item by being aware of its location at all times. While traveling, it is essential to always stay vigilant. Do not keep all your money in one place; divide your cash and credit cards in case they are lost or stolen.

Figure 6.1 Pickpockets Are Found in Every
Country. Always Be on Guard.

(4) Safety Risks: Keep up to date with the news when overseas.

Every country or region is different, and some situations are more fluid than others. Incidents involving terrorism, political unrest, natural disasters, or the outbreak of a virus can evolve quickly, so you will need to stay abreast of both domestic and international developments.

While abroad, check for travel warnings or alerts (which you automatically receive if registered with STEP), visit the websites for the Centers for Disease Control (CDC) or World Health Organization (WHO), read local newspapers, talk to the hotel staff or your hosts about what is happening in the area, write down the address of the US Consulate or Embassy, stay in contact with your travel organizer and family, and monitor international developments. Always have a rally point in case of an emergency, whether at a host member's house, a hotel, or a US government building.

4 Responses to Risks

Now that you have identified all possible risks, prioritized them, and sought to mitigate them, it is helpful to briefly discuss other ways of handling them. We will do so by organizing our responses into four verbs that all begin with "a": avoid, allocate, alleviate, and assume. Although alleviating, or mitigating, risks is perhaps most common, there are several ways to respond to a likely and/or impactful risk.

(1) Avoid the Risk

Depending on the likelihood and impact of the potential risk, you may be able to avoid it altogether. For example, you may have been planning to spend part of your trip to South Africa in Johannesburg, but, because of the high likelihood and impact of terrorist activity, you decide to skip Johannesburg and instead visit other safer areas of the country.

(2) Allocate the Risk

Some risks can be allocated or transferred to another entity. For instance, if you would like to rent horses for the weekend in Argentina but are concerned about being financially liable should they sustain an injury, you can allocate the risk by purchasing insurance that protects you from this financial threat. If something unfortunate does occur, the bulk of risk will have been allocated to the insurance provider.

(3) Alleviate the Risk

As mentioned above, alleviating or mitigating risk is the most common way of dealing with it. It can also overlap with allocation of risk. In general, alleviating risk is all about lessening or diminishing either the likelihood and/or impact of a risk. For example, if you were planning on going scuba diving for the first time during your trip to Australia, you could alleviate the risks involved by becoming certified to scuba dive in your home country months before your trip, by learning the ocean pattens where you will dive in Australia, and by asking the scuba diver in charge to stay close to you when under water.

(4) Assume the Risk

If you have rated a risk as very likely but of very low impact, you may want to consider just assuming or accepting it. For instance, let's say you are planning to spend the whole day sightseeing in Rio de Janeiro, Brazil. All of your friends have said that purses are frequently stolen there, but you still want to wear one so that you have a place to keep your water bottle and snack. Because you have decided that the purse itself has little value and you have removed all valuables from it—knowing that it could get stolen—you assume the risk of having it taken because all you have in it is water and a granola bar, so it is of little significance if it were snatched.

Conclusion

Risk is everywhere in life, and it is especially common in international travel. However, the good news is that there are many ways to measure risk and respond to it. By putting into practice the acronym RISK, by quantitatively measuring the likelihood and impact of risk, and by taking to heart the four ways to deal with it when it arrives, you will be much better prepared for any threats that might come your way when traveling overseas. As always, be safe and consult with others when you are uncertain about something.

Reflection Questions

1. Would you ever travel into a country with a Level 3 or Level 4 designation?

2. What kind of risk do you fear most or least: health, economic, or security?

3. What items would be of great enough value that you would keep on your persons at all times?

4. When you traveled in the past, was a rally point designated in case of emergency? How much safer would you have felt knowing there was such a place?

5. How might traveling with children or in a group change your risk assessment?

CHAPTER 7
CONTINGENCY PLANNING

Contingencies in Cuba

The day I arrived in Havana, Cuba, an extremely powerful hurricane was forming in the Caribbean, wreaking havoc on smaller islands and headed straight for Cuba's second largest city. I had to figure out how to respond quickly. Traveling to Cuba in October, "the season" for hurricanes, I was prepared for what was to follow and had a backup plan available, recognizing that a Plan B or even Plan C can quickly become a Plan A in this day and age of travel. As it turned out, the hurricane turned eastward and never hit Cuba as meteorologists had predicted, but it is still better to create a contingency plan that is never needed than encounter a disaster that is not anticipated.

Always Have A "Plan B" in Place

I have written previously about logistics coordination, travel insurance, and risk management. Those topics generally encompass other items that require immediate responses, such as theft, injury, or illness. As such, they will not be covered here. For the time being, I would like to briefly discuss a related item: contingency plans. Developing a contingency plan, otherwise known as "Plan B," is a non-negotiable in today's global climate. Unfortunately, hardly a news cycle breaks that does not contain some mention of a forest fire or famine, an outbreak of Ebola or a novel strand of the flu, a protest against the government or armed rebels invading a capital, or a foreigner who is arrested for stealing or violating some unknown law. Although we are not living in the Apocalypse, it can sure seem that way when watching international news.

Below, in the context of the 5 most likely emergencies you could encounter when traveling abroad, I suggest 5 steps to follow, each beginning with the letter "i": (1) investigate, (2) identify, (3) implement, (4) inform, and (5) itemize. By following these steps, you will have a solid contingency plan in place that can save you and others from possible harm when traveling.

Figure 7.1 The First Time I Went to Quito, Ecuador,
I Experienced an Earthquake. Natural Disasters
Happen Every Day in Some Part of the World.

Disasters

Earthquakes, forest fires, hurricanes, storms, floods. They happen every day in some part of the world, and, if you travel frequently enough, you will probably experience one of them firsthand. The first day I arrived in Quito, Ecuador, for instance, the country registered a sizeable earthquake in the central part of the country.

Step 1: Investigate. When preparing for a trip overseas, *investigate* everything about your destination, including its geography, climate, and weather patterns.

Earthquakes are not an uncommon occurrence in this part of the world, and so, in my planning, I had given the possibility of an earthquake a low yet possible chance of occurrence. What I was not able to know for certain, though, was the degree of impact an earthquake may or may not have on our travel plans. I estimated that an earthquake with a magnitude of less than five or six would not seriously jeopardize our plans. As it turned out, the earthquake registered a magnitude of a little more than six, and so it did not do as much damage as it could have. We were fortunate that we did not have to rearrange any of our plans, and no one from our group was even remotely impacted.

Terrorism

When I prepare a group for a trip to Israel, security is foremost in everyone's mind. Images of rockets being fired from Gaza or clashes between settlers and Palestinians flash through people's minds, and I understand their concern.

Step 2: Identify. Upon investigating your international destination, including all recent news, *identify* the three most serious scenarios that could unfold. Rank these scenarios according to (a) likelihood of occurrence and (b) impact of occurrence.

One possibility that I have to always plan for when going to Israel is terrorism. It is, of course, something we never want to occur, but a traveler has to plan for what could happen, especially if a group is involved. I identify and discuss the possibility of terrorism with my Middle East groups and give directions about how to respond in the event that terrorism occurs while we are traveling. In general, groups respond much better to a crisis if you have already given them warning and a plan to follow.

Outbreak

We were scheduled to be in Puerto Rico at the height of the Zika Virus outbreak in the winter of 2016. Travelers were canceling their confirmed reservations left and right, but our airline refused to alter our flights, maintaining that the Zika Virus outbreak was not covered under our insurance plan. We were left with two options: (i) Lose most of our trip investment or (ii) continue with our trip and implement a contingency plan while there.

Step 3: Implement. Upon identifying the greatest threats possible in your destination, *implement* a clear, simple, and succinct contingency plan.

We eventually chose the second option after identifying all the health risks and implementing a solid and safe way to mitigate them. Our implementation of the plan called for a rearrangement of the places we were going to visit—staying clear of all the mosquito hot spots on the island, aggressively applying mosquito repellent, wearing protective clothing, and exercising increased levels of caution every day. Happily, despite the extreme measures we took, everyone ended up having a safe and enjoyable trip.

Unrest

I was preparing a university trip to Hong Kong when social protests against the government began to escalate in the summer and fall of 2019. Monitoring the situation closely, I began crafting two contingency plans to communicate to travel participants: (i) a backup destination and (ii) specific instructions about how to respond to civil unrest if experienced in-country.

Step 4: Inform. Upon implementing a contingency plan for your destination, *inform* all shareholders in the most effective way possible.

By informing everyone about your contingency plans, you are not only showing good foresight, but you are also keeping yourself accountable when the unthinkable does occur.

Detainment

I was preparing a group for Turkey at a time when a prominent American citizen was being detained in a Turkish prison. Tensions were running high, and one person planning to travel with us began making threats about bringing a gun to Turkey and openly violating Turkish laws.

Step 5: Itemize. Upon informing all shareholders of a contingency plan, you must *itemize* and document any enactments of the contingency plan, especially those relating to legal or ethical violations.

Unfortunately, we had to prohibit the person from traveling with us. Group leaders cannot knowingly put the safety and security of travelers in harm's way, especially when avoidable. In high-risk countries, leaders must consider the possibility that someone could get arrested. Ideally, the risks should be mitigated before departing by clearly explaining acceptable and unacceptable behavior when traveling; however, if detainment or arrest does occur when in-country, a plan needs to be put in place detailing how you will respond.

An Example: IF/THEN

When creating your contingency plans, be as specific as possible. Write out the most likely emergencies that could occur by ranking them according to likelihood of occurrence and impact of occurrence, with clear action items listed beside them. Naturally, the higher the likelihood and impact of occurrence, the more aggressive the action you need to take. Devise the plan as an IF/THEN statement. For instance, IF someone from your group is arrested overseas, THEN you will do the following.

Contingency Plan for Detainment: IF someone is detained or arrested overseas, THEN follow these 5 steps: (1) contact the US Embassy or Consulate in that country, ideally speaking with someone on the phone or in person; (2) if you are part of an official tour, report it to the organization's leader; (3) notify the contact person listed for the detained traveler; (4) hire an attorney, preferably one that you or your organization has an existing relationship with; and (5) document exactly what happened to keep for your records.

Conclusion

It goes without saying that none of wants to imagine a long-anticipated international trip to result in a natural disaster or civil rest, for instance, but these extreme cases do occur more often than realized. To prepare yourself and anyone traveling with you for possible emergency situations, it is essential that sound, reasonable, and detailed contingency plans are established that can be implemented on the spot.

To be sure, even after following the five steps above, it is important to note that other scenarios can also occur and that your contingency plans may lead to unexpected costs, tough decisions, and lots of paperwork. But it is better to have something in place that may not be exact than nothing at all. Take a cue from airlines: The first thing they provide on each and every flight is a clear explanation about how to respond if the flight were to necessitate an emergency landing. Foresight goes a long way. And, when traveling internationally, it can save your life.

Reflection Questions

1. List each of the "i" words mentioned in this chapter. Which do you think is most important?

2. What would a "Plan B" likely be if you couldn't travel where you originally thought?

3. Are you prepared to keep a person from traveling if they act or speak in ways that imperil the group?

4. What would your IF/THEN scenario look like?

5. Is there an attorney you know that would be available if needed on an international trip?

CHAPTER 8
GETTING PACKED

A Porter in Palestine

We were about a week into our trip in Israel and the West Bank. Walking through the war-torn town of Hebron, in the West Bank (or Palestine) in the heat of the day, I found myself carrying two heavy bags for hours as we toured both the Israeli and Palestinian sides of the town. Our visits were incredible and very eye-opening, but I was constantly having to readjust the bags I was carrying, which only worsened as I, the tour leader, needed to stop at a store on a couple of occasions to purchase water and snacks for the group. And worst of all, neither of the heavy bags I was carrying were my own—they were the bags of two travelers who had insisted on bringing them but were now too exhausted to carry them on their own. If only they had listened to my consistent advice to limit their luggage and keep unnecessary items at home or in their hotel rooms.

The Most Coveted Item in Travel

In all my years of leading groups, there's one item more requested than any other: a packing list. In my early days of organizing trips, I sent information about packing last. After all, I naively reasoned, packing isn't urgent, and travelers can wait for a checklist until *after* receiving more important information about passports, flights, and vaccinations. Although I don't think I was wrong, I now send a packing checklist to travelers as soon as possible. And why wouldn't I?

Anticipation Is Golden

For many travelers, the anticipation of a trip is almost as

exciting as the trip itself. This makes perfect sense. For me, preparing for a trip is like getting ready for the Christmas season. Putting up lights, decorating a Christmas tree, buying presents, and watching holiday classics—that is almost as much fun as Christmas Day.

In a similar way, a lot of travelers like to prepare for an upcoming trip by purchasing luggage, buying needed accessories, and shopping for new outfits. For travelers such as these, sending a packing list as soon as they register for a trip is a wonderful way to get them excited for what is to come, even if it's still months away.

General Advice: Keep Luggage to a Minimum

Let's start with the basics. How many bags should you take, and exactly what size bags are we talking about? The decision is ultimately up to you, but I recommend limiting luggage to the essentials.

Although your luggage will mostly be confined to the airplane, your hotel room, and transportation to and from, you will still need to carry it more than expected: in and through airports, to and from a bus, train, or taxi, inside and outside of your hotel accommodations, uphill and downhill, and many places in between. I speak from experience when I write that there is nothing glamorous about lugging around giant suitcases; they're heavy, difficult to navigate on curbs, stairs, and escalators, and they take up a lot of space—a precious commodity when leaving the United States.

I suggest limiting your luggage to one 9" x 21" x 14" carry-on bag and one personal item, such as a backpack or handbag. The airline industry continues to cut every corner, and I see no reason to pay extra money for luggage that I can store in an overhead bin, or that the airlines could potentially misdirect or even lose. Besides, when traveling light, you have more mobility, you stick out less in a crowd, and you do not require extra services from drivers and porters, who will require a tip if they have to handle your luggage.

The World Is at Your Fingertips—Even When Abroad

It's not uncommon for travelers to bring twice the number of items they need when traveling. They do so under the illusion that they will actually wear 2 or 3 outfits a day. However, the truth of the matter is that many travelers only wear 1 outfit a day, which can be shed or added to if you wear clothes in layers—as I heartily recommend you do. Instead of bringing extra clothes, plan realistically and question whether you will really wear that shirt in the back of your closet that you haven't donned in 3 years. Also, believe it or not, there is no international law that you can't wear the same pants 2 days in a row—or even more. If so, I would have been arrested years ago.

In a related way, some travelers overpack because they assume other countries do not sell toiletries, snacks, and cosmetic supplies. I do recommend, of course, bringing your own toothbrush, deodorant, hygiene products, and other such toiletries. But you do not need extras. Due to globalization, most countries have the exact—or very similar—kinds of products you have back home. I recommend bringing only what you really need and leaving the rest to purchases you can make at a convenient store, pharmacy, or supermarket when overseas. Depending on which country you are visiting, you may actually be able to find a product at a better rate—and it's also a lot of fun buying products unique to a country.

Long story short: Umbrellas, sunblock, socks, pens, adapters, headphones, Tylenol, tissues, Tampons, toothpaste, sweatshirts, sandals—every country has them, so don't stress if you have to buy something when overseas. That's part of the fun of traveling.

The ABCs of Clothing

The ABCs of clothing are (a) **a**ppropriate, (b) **b**reathable, and (c) **c**omfortable.

Figure 8.1 When Packing for a Trip, Follow the ABCs of Clothing.

(A) Appropriate

Clothing that is *appropriate* possesses 2 traits. First, it's culturally appropriate, meaning that you do not, for example, wear seductive clothing in a traditional and conservative society. Be sure to respect the culture and try not to attract unnecessary attention to yourself. Also, it's important to remember that historic sites, museums, and government buildings may require a certain dress code; learn what that is before you board your plane or, at least, before you leave your hotel that day. And it goes without saying that clothing for women and men is different. Depending on your exact destination, and I lead a lot of trips to places with traditional values, societies apply stricter standards for women's clothing, such as expecting women to wear something covering their shoulders and legs, especially at religious sites. For women, scarves are excellent additions to your luggage, so be sure to always bring one along. Second, *appropriate* clothing contains that which is suitable for the weather and climate you will be visiting. If you are traveling to India in the summer, for instance, you probably don't need a coat. However, if you are visiting England—even in the summer—a raincoat will probably be needed.

(B) Breathable

By "breathable," I am referring to clothing that can be easily aired out and reused without being too heavy or needing too much time to dry. When on the road, after all, wearing clothing that is breathable will allow you to wash it in your sink (or in a bucket if camping outdoors), air it out overnight, and still make use of it the next day—if you so choose. (By the way, all major hotels provide laundering services for a fee, or you can bring detergent packets to wash clothing in your hotel room.) And if the weather is warm, which it often is in the high season of travel, breathable clothing will help you stay cooler.

(C) Comfortable

Comfort speaks for itself in most situations, but especially when wearing clothes for fifteen hours a day, and possibly for several days in a short amount of time. For some reason, people love buying new shoes or sandals for an international trip, only to discover that they cause foot blisters or are uncomfortable. I recommend only bringing tried-and-true footwear on trips—shoes you KNOW are comfortable and able to withstand extreme use. Go ahead and wear out your old shoes on your trip, and plan to purchase new shoes when you are back home.

What If I Can't Live without the Internet?

I write elsewhere about social media and international travel, but the bottom line is that most people can't survive without the internet. I get it, and you can be rest assured that most places you visit provide internet access. Nowadays, practically all hotels offer Wi-Fi access, though it can be limited, restricted to the lobby, or only available for purchase. When out and about, many public places provide Wi-Fi services. For communicating to people on your trip and at home, I use WhatsApp. You can download this app on your phone free of charge. WhatsApp provides free phone calls, video chats, and text messages once you have an internet connection. Elsewhere, I also write about purchasing a travel plan with your cell phone provider, which will enable you to have phone, text, and internet coverage when traveling overseas.

Laptops and Tablets

There is nothing that ruins your trip like a laptop or tablet that is lost or stolen. And what's worse, the average traveler does not always need these items. To be sure, everyone is different, and I understand that tablets double over as TVs, cameras, phones, and desktops; but think carefully before bringing any major electronics on an international trip. I rarely bring anything more than a phone, since it will allow me to do most anything a tablet can do, and it's much harder for me to forget my cell phone somewhere or have it stolen. If you do decide to bring a laptop or tablet, take the necessary precautions:

- Make sure it has a very firm casing that can withstand being dropped or stepped on.

- Create a passcode and always use it.

- Be incredibly careful about your internet connection; it could be public, meaning that others could attempt to access your information without your knowledge.

- When not in use, keep it in a safe or other secure place. If I bring a tablet with me, it's always in my hotel safe unless in use.

- Always carry a backup cord. If you lose your cord or it's stolen, your laptop or tablet could be useless if you don't have one.

Adapters and Convertors

One last thing when it comes to electronics: Most countries use a different electrical system than the US. While American appliances run on 110 volts, many other countries do not. Be sure to do a search online to determine what type of voltage is needed where you are visiting. Fortunately, most devices these days offer dual voltage, which means you only need to purchase an adapter to ensure your device will be charged when overseas.

What about Money?

Should you use a credit card or cash overseas? It depends. In Scandinavian countries, for instance, you can purchase almost anything with your credit card; in less developed countries, however, cash is preferred, if not required. In general, I recommend making as many purchases as possible with your credit card (the one with the "chip" is ideal), as credit cards often have the best exchange rates and no foreign transaction fees. Of course, you will want to inform your credit card provider beforehand of your travel dates and destinations. For those who would like to carry pocket change in the local currency, there are many ways it can be obtained:

- Withdraw local currency out of your debit card from ATMs (not credit cards), which are available at all airports and within close proximity to hotels and city centers.

- Bring your local currency and change it at banks and exchange houses, which are available at all airports and near major tourist sites.

- Exchange your currency at hotels (many hotels are able to make small exchanges).

In some public places, use of bathrooms requires cash, so it is best to always have the equivalent of a few dollars for the use of bathroom facilities, tips, subway tickets, or snacks.

Prescriptions and Medications

It goes without saying that prescription medication is probably the most important item you might carry in your luggage. When traveling overseas, be sure to keep your prescription medication in the bottle you received it in, request at least a week's extra in case you face a travel interruption, and leave it in a bag you have ready access to (not in a checked bag). Worst case scenario, it is possible to get prescription medication overseas, but bringing it with you is ideal. For over-the-counter medication, plan to bring whatever you think may be needed: something for a headache, upset stomach, or motion sickness. For everything else—from allergies to an unexpected UTI infection—you will likely be able to find it in-country.

Unlike the US, for instance, pharmacies in other countries usually provide knowledgeable staff members who can help you find the right medication for your ailment. Simply describe your condition to someone at a pharmacy and look online for the main ingredient in the drug you would use back home. What's best, in most countries outside the US, the pharmacy will allow you to purchase only what you need, not buy an entire packet. Finally, be sure to also bring along prescription glasses or contact lenses. And if you wear prescription sunglasses, carry those in a protective covering so that they do not break or crack when traveling.

Last but Not Least: TSA Regulations

The TSA regulates that all liquids must be in a bottle 100 ml (3.4 ounces) or less. Anything greater will be confiscated and discarded. This applies to virtually ALL liquids—shampoo, lotion, water, perfume, mouth wash, you name it. If your bottle contains more than 3.4 ounces, you will not be able to take it with you. For any snacks you pack, make sure they are placed in a clear bag that can be easily separated from your other items.

Conclusion

Before going on any international trip, create a packing list with care, keeping in mind the items mentioned above. Like Santa Claus, I recommend checking the list twice, but be especially nice to yourself if you discover that you forgot something when you arrive overseas. Nobody is perfect, and after twenty years of leading international trips, I also sometimes forget items I intended to pack.

Reflection Questions

1. Could you see yourself purchasing a new outfit or suitcase for an upcoming trip?

2. Does the thought of limiting your baggage intimidate you or does it bring freedom?

3. What were the ABCs of clothing? Does or should this translate at all for how to dress in your home country?

4. What precautions are mentioned for laptops and tablets? Would you personally risk bringing one?

5. How do pharmacies differ overseas from in the United States? Overall, how can a flexible mindset overcome lost, forgotten, or misplaced items?

CHAPTER 9
PHYSICAL READINESS

Hiking in Mexico

We were well into our trip to Mexico, and now we found ourselves spending a few days in the Yucatan Peninsula. However, I could tell that a couple of the group members were becoming physically weary. Although they started off strong in Mexico City despite long days and lots of walking through city streets, cultural museums, and historic churches, they were now exhausted. And, so, after the first day of hiking, they decided to stay back in the hotel for the next day, missing out on what turned out to be the group's most exciting part of the entire itinerary.

Physical Health

The physical rigors of travel extend well beyond jet lag, a topic I later devote an entire chapter to. Depending on your age, health condition, and the kind of journey you are undertaking, you will need to attend to your body before ever stepping foot on a plane. In this chapter, we will isolate the elements necessary to get in the best possible physical condition while traveling. Please believe me when I say that being at your optimal health before departing will serve you in countless ways on your journey overseas.

(1) Become Active

As simple as it sounds, one of the best ways you can prepare for your trip is to get in the habit of walking regularly. As the saying goes, "practice makes perfect." Where should you walk? For those who want to simulate a "typical" overseas trip, I recommend walking across all kinds of terrains: alongside downtown streets, through museums, at parks, up hills, down staircases, and on dirt roads. And, if possible, all in the same shoes you will wear on your trip. (As I mentioned in the previous chapter, never wear shoes for the first time on an overseas trip unless you are prepared for the consequences: blisters, band aids, and generally unhappy feet.) In the end, it matters less where you walk and more that you walk. Every step you take today will aid you tomorrow.

Ignore at Your Own Peril

In addition to walking, you may also want to consider other kinds of exercise, whether weightlifting, jogging, cycling, spinning, playing sports, dancing, or pursuing other aerobic activities. Once again, what is most important is that you are adopting a more active lifestyle and preparing your body for the journey ahead. I have witnessed countless travelers ignore this advice only to regret it afterward. While overseas, they gradually come to terms with the physical rigors of travel and thereby skip planned visits, cut short their daily excursions, or retire for the evening before everyone else does. To be sure, no one expects a traveler to be in perfect health or at the prime of his or her life, but you would be surprised at how weeks or months of physical preparation before a trip—even if that means walking on a treadmill for twenty minutes a day—can assist someone while abroad.

Remember the Example of Peggy

I remember one of my travelers several years ago named Peggy. She was eighty-two years old. While registering for the trip, she confided that she was nervous about her physical health due to her age. But after discussing some exercises she could to do prepare months before the trip—in consultation with her doctor, of course—she arrived on the plane with a spryness that surpassed people half her age. For the entire duration of the trip, Peggy held strong, never missed one activity, and often fared better than some of our travelers in their twenties and thirties.

Figure 9.1 Travelers Do More Walking Than Expected When Traveling Overseas. The More in Shape You Are, the Better.

(2) Eat Healthy

I mention elsewhere that one of the most exciting features of international travel is the new and exotic food options available. Are you interested in eating scorpion on a stick? It is amply available in certain East Asian countries. Or would you instead prefer to eat guinea pig on a stick, something sold in South America? If you are horrified by the prospect of eating either, don't cancel your trip just yet. Because of globalization, most countries today carry staples that most people are familiar with. You will be just fine.

However, before you begin to focus on what you will eat overseas, I encourage you to consider your diet while at home. In general, doctors and dieticians recommend a diet heavy in fruits and vegetables, low in processed foods, and combined with the optimal mixture of proteins like chicken and fish, and fibers like beans, lentils, and whole grains. Set yourself up for success by keeping away—even if just the week prior to your trip—from fried foods, sugary drinks, pastries, and other items that tend to weigh you down rather than lift you up. You will want to start your trip on the right foot, and that means taking care of your body and monitoring what you eat. And don't forget that your trip begins on the airplane, thousands of feet above ground, which environment can easily upset your stomach, so be kind to it before you board.

(3) Visit Your Physician

It is always recommended to schedule an appointment with your physician before an international trip. This is especially the case depending on your age, preexisting health conditions, and destination. Your doctor can determine which exercises you can reasonably perform to get in better shape, what medications you may need, and what vaccinations may be required. If you have any health concerns at all, resolve them with your personal physician *before* going overseas. For instance, I have had some travelers who needed a procedure before their trip, but they decided to delay the procedure until afterward. On the trip, however, what started off as minor pain sometimes escalated into something more painful. If at all possible, and depending on the nature of the medical procedure, I recommend undergoing those procedures before you travel—ideally, weeks or month before—so that you do not experience any discomfort while away. As much as you are able, you want to travel overseas when you are in prime health.

(4) Boost Your Immune System

Before you go airborne, get Airborne. Or consider similar vitamins, minerals, antioxidants, herbs, or supplements that can boost your body's ability to cope with germs at airports and on airplanes. You don't want to arrive to your international destination sick from something that could have been avoided or, at least, mitigated. Despite its mostly negative qualities, one of the positive outcomes of COVID-19 is that it has prompted travelers to be very proactive when it comes to their health.

I remember a trip I once took to South Korea. We started in Philadelphia the night before, taking an early-morning flight to Detroit, then catching a layover in Los Angeles before heading directly to Seoul. By the time I arrived, I was feeling horrible, partly because of jet lag and partly because I must have picked up something at an airport or on one of the planes.

When I leave for an international trip, I begin boosting my immune system several days beforehand. I drink a lot of water, eat a good portion of vegetables and fruits, regulate my sleep, exercise every day, and take supplements, Vitamin C, and sometimes the antioxidant elderberry. Although some debate the medicinal effectiveness of such supplements, I continue to use them for several reasons: They do not do any harm, they remind me to take my health seriously, and they put me in the right frame of mind for travel.

(5) Stick to Your Diet

When I first starting leading trips decades ago, meals were designed mostly for mass consumption. People had few options. Today, however, things are much different—though, of course, it completely depends on your destination. In many countries today, restaurants and supermarkets readily offer vegetarian, vegan, and gluten-free options. When ordering food for groups, I can almost always find a way to satisfy travelers who may be on special diets. If you would like to stick to your diet while traveling, here are 5 tips you can follow.

1. **Pack your own snacks as much as possible:** Before I leave for an international trip, I collect all the food that I want to have available for snacks and I keep these in a separate bag. Non-perishable items like nuts, dried fruit, protein bars, oatmeal, and beef jerky can be lifesavers when hunger pains strike before lunch or after physical

activity, and they never spoil while traveling. To me, it makes perfect sense to have available snacks that my body craves, that it's used to, and that are easy to carry. Also, on the day of my trip, I always pack a meal in a brown bag that I keep with me. Sometimes it serves as my dinner at the airport, sometimes as my breakfast on the plane (depending on what is offered, if anything), and sometimes I save it for a snack once I arrive in-country. You may also want to consider bringing along more substantive food items that you can pack in your checked luggage.

2. **When possible, purchase food at supermarkets and cook it yourself:** This is one of the definite perks of choosing Airbnb or staying in a place that has a kitchen. You can choose the food that works best for you, and it's also usually cheaper than eating out. Good items to purchase overseas, assuming you have no allergies to them, are yogurt, fruits with an outer skin, canned vegetables, rice, beans, and granola. In general, I think it's a good thing to give your body something familiar at least once a day when traveling overseas. Traveling is jarring enough. You want to keep your body as happy as possible.

3. **Reduce your food intake:** On trips that I lead, it's not uncommon for travelers to gain weight, despite the heavy amount of walking we do. How so? Depending on the trip, we often eat breakfast and dinners at the hotel buffet, where everything and anything is available. And even during lunches, some of the most convenient places for tourists happen to offer buffet meals. With so much food available, people can be tempted to overeat, or eat two or three desserts a day. Sometimes, when traveling alone or with friends or family, I eat a large breakfast, skip lunch, and then opt for an early dinner.

4. **Eat vegetables and fruit at every meal:** I recommend filling up on vegetables and fruit before going for less nutritious options afterward. Hopefully, by prioritizing the good stuff, you will have less room or appetite for the bad stuff. To be sure, you definitely want to try new foods and take advantage of unique treats you will encounter overseas; but try to fill up on foods that put your body in ideal health.

5. **Keep hydrated:** As I will mention when I discuss jet lag in a separate chapter, your body is likely dehydrated by the time you arrive in-country. Most people do not drink enough water as it is, let alone while at the airport or on the airplane. And with the low humidity conditions present on most airplanes, the likelihood of dehydration only increases. Although I lament the high cost of bottled water at airports (and even on planes), drinking water helps with digestion, enhances your mood, assists appetite control, and generally promotes a healthy mind and body. And because a lot of international travel involves walking (and/or spending time in the sun or heat), one of the most important things you can do on your trip is to remain as hydrated as possible. In short, always keep a bottle of water available.

Conclusion

Although simple advice, the more you can take care of your body before your trip (and, of course, during it), the better kind of trip you are destined to have. After all, international travel is a full-body experience—engaging every aspect of who you are as a person—so it only makes sense that the physical plays an extremely important role. As discussed above, there are many ways that you can optimize your health. But if you want to start small, for instance, by simply establishing walking goals for yourself, consider Julie Ann Price's *The Walking Challenge:*

Before You Go Overseas

Reap the Health Benefits of Walking. As I mentioned above, walking may be the single greatest activity you do while preparing for international travel.

Reflection Questions

1. What physical training regimen would you consider adopting before you travel overseas?

2. Which of your usual foods should you forego before traveling?

3. If you were to visit your doctor today, what would he or she say about your physical health?

4. Traveling sick can be a nightmare. What specific ways can you boost your immune system before your trip?

5. Have you ever tried calculating how much water you drink per day? Talk to your doctor and come up with a plan, so you can remain at peak hydration.

CHAPTER 10
CULTURAL ELEMENTS

Understanding the Culture of Germany

It wasn't until the fifth time I visited Germany that I began to really understand its culture. This is despite the fact that I have German ancestry, I studied German history, language, and culture for my PhD, and I had visited the country over the course of several years. Understanding all the different components that comprise a culture, after all, is not an easy task, nor is it a swift one. Things only began to crystallize for me during this fifth visit—when I was briefly living in the country—at which time I was able to see, feel, and experience the German way of life first-hand.

What Is Culture?

Culture is a constellation of forces shaping a society. It is not one thing in particular, but a combination of elements seemingly unrelated but ultimately melded together to forge an identity: history and politics, laws and economics, race and sexuality, art and media, sports and entertainment, religion and spirituality, food and drink, language and behaviors, and much more besides. A living force, culture is always changing and always being shaped by people and circumstances, yet it cannot never be fully controlled.

Avoiding Ethnocentrism

When traveling overseas, you will have to constantly be on guard against the mental mapping that has framed your cultural understanding of what is "right" and what is "wrong." This is difficult to counteract since most people assume their way is "the" way of doing something, which means that the opposite way must be incorrect, askew, or at least suspect. If you grew up in America, for instance, you automatically have a predisposition to how decisions should be made (individually or personally), what rights you should be afforded (all rights promoting liberty and freedom), and what opportunities should be made available to you (most all of them). However, should you find yourself visiting or living in another country, you may find that the people living there think and feel quite differently about such matters.

Leaning In

Because culture is comprised of so many different forces, there is no silver bullet to understanding how a culture operates. Nor is it possible for a person to completely come to terms with a culture by visiting it once or even many times. Still, trying to understand culture is one of the many reasons people spend so much time and money traveling overseas, and the sooner you attempt to lean into the culture you are visiting, the better off you will be. Please note that leaning in is not the same thing as blindly accepting. Without doubt, some cultural attitudes and behaviors you encounter overseas are demeaning or downright reprehensible, so I am not suggesting you forgo your religious and ethical values when traveling abroad.

Between the extremes of ethnocentric pride and cultural relativism lie a space that aims to be humble, teachable, respectful, and charitable. Below is my recipe for leaning into your cultural experience.
1. **Be humble:** Acknowledge your own shortcomings. Admit you do not know everything.
2. **Be teachable:** Take a learning posture. Act like you are a student in a classroom.
3. **Be respectful:** Give honor where honor is due. Remember that *you* are the guest.

4. **Be charitable:** Choose the high road. Give the benefit of the doubt.
5. **Be realistic:** Accept the cultural divide between you and your host culture. Locals know you are not a native.

Learn about These Cultural Elements before Going Abroad

The list of components below is not exhaustive, but it's a start. As a Westerner, I naturally think in practice-and-theory terms, and so my recommendation is to become acquainted with as many of the components as possible, whether through practice or theory. And it's important to note that I am not talking about reading academic books or taking a graduate class to learn this information. Start small and choose the medium you prefer: Download an app that teaches you the basics of Swahili, rent an Israeli movie with English subtitles, read a Wikipedia article on Brazilian rain forests, watch a documentary about how Japanese chefs prepare sushi, find a blog describing the best beaches in Australia, view a YouTube clip of the leading museums in France, or check out a cookbook with Indian recipes. It's that simple, and below are the categories you can begin exploring.

History and Politics

Before you travel overseas, consider reading a book about the history of your destination. This can be an in-depth treatment or, more realistically, a short article online or even a blog. I also recommend becoming familiar with the country's form of government and even learning about some of its government leaders.

Fun Fact: Politics in Finland: When I was preparing for a trip to Finland, I learned that the prime minister's coalition government (including the prime minister herself) is comprised exclusively of females, the majority of whom at the time were under forty.

Before You Go Overseas

Laws and Economics

Few people would want to study the GDP (Gross Domestic Product) of a country they are visiting, but you may want to review the CIA World Factbook, which contains a brief summary of major economic items connected to any country you visit. Likewise, I recommend the US Department of State's Bureau of Consular Affairs. The "International Travel" section of this website contains excellent data about each global destination. Keep in mind that certain countries have much stricter laws than the US, so you will want to be aware of those before stepping foot in country and risking a fine or even detainment. And it goes without saying that you will want to familiarize yourself with the local currency of the country you are visiting as well as its exchange rate with the US Dollar.

Fun Fact: Economics in China: I knew China was an economic powerhouse through my study of business, but witnessing the construction first-hand, having conversations with leaders, and seeing its different enterprises left me with a much deeper understanding.

Race, Gender, Sexuality, and Family

Cultures can vary dramatically on these important topics. Some countries, for instance, are less friendly to single female travelers, while still others may be more welcoming or more condemning of same-sex couples or people from a certain race or ethnicity. Learn as much as you can before going overseas.

Fun Fact: Race in Cuba: One of the most interesting museums I ever attended was the Museum of the Revolution in Havana, Cuba, which is located inside the former mansion of the prime ministers before Fidel Castro assumed office in 1959. It was illuminating to see how the different races and historic ethnicities of Cubans worked together during the revolution.

Figure 10.1 Visiting the Museum of the Revolution in
Havana, Cuba Was an Eye-Opening Experience for Me.

Art, Literature, Media, and Architecture

One of my favorite things to experience overseas is traditional
music, dance, art, and architecture. When I was in Norway, for
instance, I fell in love with medieval stave churches, and in
Portugal, I loved listening to Fado, the traditional music in that
country where, in tiny bars, the singer pours out her heart just
inches from your table.

Fun Fact: Reading in Iceland: When traveling to Iceland,
I learned that Iceland has the most literate population in the
entire world. Book shops in the capital of Reykjavik were
everywhere, and I enjoyed visiting them and learning more
about Norse mythology.

Sports and Entertainment

Every country has its own national sport and form of
entertainment. When at all possible, consider attending a

professional or semi-professional sports match or some other event in which you get to experience another layer of the culture. This means attending a cricket match when visiting Australia or New Zealand, a soccer match when visiting most of Europe and Latin America, or some kind of music, art, or dancing concert or public fair in any destination. The more unique the public event, the better.

Fun Fact: Bullfighting in Spain: One of the most interesting experiences in my travels was attending a bull fight in the Plaza de los Toros de Las Ventas in Madrid, Spain, probably the most famous bullring in the world. I can't say I enjoyed what I saw, but it was an experience I will never forget.

Clothing and Fashion

One thing I love doing overseas is visiting shoe stores. Although there are certain brands that are sold everywhere, each region has its own style of shoe. Some emphasize color, some design, some comfort, and still others emphasize something else. The same goes for clothing, hairstyles, and jewelry.

Fun Fact: Sock Shopping in Korea: I always try to buy a pair of unique socks when traveling overseas. Where's the best place to buy them? At the local market or at a vendor underground in the subway. Seoul, Korea, like many other great cities, has an extensive subway system, which also contains lots of shops. One of my favorite socks are the orange ones I purchased for less than $1. Because Koreans remove their shoes before going inside a person's home, the designs of their socks are a big deal.

Religion and Spirituality

All countries have a traditional religion, which shapes the culture in profound ways. I encourage you to visit a local house of worship when overseas and even do a little reading beforehand. Some of my most meaningful travel experiences have occurred at local religious sites.

Fun Fact: Religions in Singapore: Probably the most accessible place to see world religions in action is Singapore. All the major world religions are practiced under the full protection of the law and within close proximity to each other; in a short amount of time, you can learn first-hand about Buddhism, Christianity, Hinduism, Islam, Jainism, Judaism, and Sikhism. The people are welcoming, and some of the impressive buildings where the religions are practiced are worth the visit itself.

Food and Drink

What is the fun of visiting a country but never trying its most distinct dishes and drinks? Although I am not a foodie, I do relish in the prospect of eating some fabulous dish in an exotic location. I can easily list the top meals of my life, all of which occurred overseas—gelato in Italy, stew in Egypt, turkey in Turkey, cheese in Greece, freshly squeezed juice in Latin America, pretzels and beer in Bavaria, and kanafeh in Israel and Palestine.

Fun Fact: Iguana in Peru: Some Spanish-speaking countries sell iguana as food. I have seen it sold by vendors grilled on a stick in such places as Peru, Mexico, and Puerto Rico. In case you are wondering, it doesn't taste like chicken— more like alligator.

Language and Non-Verbal Communication

Although there are thousands of languages spoken today, the overwhelming amount of communication across societies occurs through body language. Basic emotions like happiness, surprise, anger, confusion, fear, and sadness are rather easily understood, so do not be anxious if you do not speak the language of the country you are visiting. At the same time, I always encourage people to learn five non-negotiable words and phrases in any language: (1) "hello," (2) "goodbye," (3) "thank you," (4) "yes," and (5) "no." Before you travel, download an app on your phone or watch a video on YouTube that teaches these most basic of words and phrases. Trust me: They will go a long way.

Before You Go Overseas

Fun Fact: Pronunciation in Poland: Many foreign alphabets can be learned faster than realized. When I travel to a country where I am unfamiliar with the alphabet, for example, I can oftentimes learn it in a few days. By learning how to pronounce Polish, for instance, I saved myself from taking the wrong train or bus on several occasions since the way Polish is pronounced can be quite different from how it looks.

Conclusion

I don't know about you, but all this talk about culture has made me incredibly grateful for the experiences I have had traveling overseas. Eating a croissant in Paris, riding a motorbike in Bangkok, attending a soccer match in Rio de Janeiro, floating in the Dead Sea in Israel—culture is the air we breathe, and having the opportunity to take part in culture is a gift that keeps on giving. Be sure to take full advantage of your next overseas trip by actively engaging the culture and participating in it rather than just observing it.

Reflection Questions

1. Culture shock can happen any time a person enters a new social environment. What culture shocks can you recall from your own experience?

2. What five attitudes should characterize a traveler when they journey abroad?

3. What is mental mapping and how do you avoid it?

4. Is there an item, like socks, that you might purposefully buy as you travel?

5. Would you eat distinct cultural foods like iguana as you travel or would you play it safe?

CHAPTER 11
CULTURAL INTELLIGENCE

South Korea Is Not East Texas

When I lived in South Korea, I was worlds apart from my American culture. Many of the values I was raised on, such as rugged individualism, treating everyone equal regardless of title, dressing casually (doesn't every culture wear cowboy boats?), and not allowing my career to dictate my schedule, were put to the test. Rather than resorting to frustration or stereotyping, however, I sought to lean into Korean culture in the recognition that I had a long way to go in my understanding of how culture shapes a society, particularly one so different from my own.

Like IQ and EQ, CQ Measures Intelligence

Culture, as previously discussed, is a constellation of forces in a society—including history, politics, religion, economics, food, language, and more. To be sure, cultures around the world share many common values and cultures. For instance, it is normal for many cultures to laud hard work, to enact laws that benefit society, and to strive to provide an excellent education for their children. But cultures can also drastically differ based on the combination of factors mentioned above. In this section, we will examine cultural intelligence, or cultural quotient (CQ), which is generally defined as the ability to successfully navigate and intelligently engage other cultures. Whereas IQ measures intellectual ability and EQ measures emotional ability, CQ measures cultural ability.

Hofstede's Cultural Consequences

Perhaps you are familiar with Geert Hofstede's work on cultural dimensions, a Dutch psychologist who conducted seminal research on cultural dimensions theory. He outlined six cultural dimensions that characterize a region, abbreviated as 6-D. Over time, Hofstede's work has been revised and modified by CQ scholars such as David Livermore and David Thomas, and I have adapted some of their insights for us to briefly review.

1. **Power Distance**: The extent to which less powerful members of organizations and institutions accept and expect that power is distributed equally or unequally.

2. **Uncertainty Avoidance:** The extent to which a culture programs its members to feel comfortable or uncomfortable in unstructured and uncertain situations.

3. **Individualism vs. Collectivism:** The extent to which individuals are expected to look after themselves (and their immediate dependents) or remain integrated societally into groups.

4. **Gender Roles:** The extent to which a society expresses its emotional and gender roles relative to one another; also referred to as "masculine vs. feminine" or "tough vs. tender" societies.

5. **Long-term vs. Short-term Orientation:** The extent to which a culture understands its time horizon relative to activities, planning, and events.

6. **Indulgence vs. Restraint:** The extent to which societies immediately accept or delay gratification of one's drives, emotions, and enjoyment of life.

7. **Low vs. High Context:** The extent to which context determines or shapes the meaning of communication and even body language.

8. **Being vs. Doing:** The extent to which contemplation and reflection play a role in a society versus action and implementation.

The US vs. South Korea in a 6-D Model

Because these dimensions work best when comparing them to another culture, I will compare how the US measures against South Korea.

Cultural Dimension	United States	South Korea
Power Distance	40	60
Individualism	91	18
Masculinity	62	39
Uncertainty Avoidance	46	85
Long-term Orientation	26	100
Indulgence	68	29
High Context	-	-
Doing vs. Being	-	-

As this simple chart illustrates, many of the cultural dimensions of both the US and South Korea are markedly different, indicating just how differently these societies will work. I will explain some of these differences below, particularly as they relate to South Korea.

(1) Likes Hierarchy: High Power Distance

To begin with, South Korea is hierarchical in its general societal structure. Like Confucian societies in general, decision making is made at the top of a family unit or organization, and subordinates are expected not to question those in authority. Saving face is important in Korea, and it would be considered very rude for subordinates to question or publicly disagree with their leaders—whether family members or bosses—and you will not usually hear the word "no" being used in response to a question. When meeting with a family or organization (such as a business or church), it is recommended to first greet the most senior member. Shaking hands is common (perhaps with a slight bow), but additional physical contact is not. Unlike an Italian culture, for instance, it is not common to hug or kiss on the cheeks.

Before You Go Overseas

(2) Prefers Groups: High Collectivism

The United States is, quite practically, the most individualistic country in the world. This is easy to forget when in the US, but it becomes very apparent when traveling to foreign countries, especially ones like South Korea that rank high on the other side: collectivism. In a collectivist society, relationships and doing things that benefit the group take much more importance than individual aims or goals. What an individual wants— which profession to enter, whom to marry, where to live—are traditionally decided by someone else. Instead, Koreans value *jeong*, "attachment" or a feeling of "affection" for family and close friends. Similarly, collectivism is easily seen in the way Korean's give their name—they will usually give their family, or last, name first, indicating their tradition and preference for aligning themselves primarily with the group. This is, of course, the exact opposite of American society, where each person has his or her own individual name that is most commonly used.

Figure 11.1 Living in South Korea Was Very Different from Living in the United States. Pay Attention to Cultural Matters When Overseas.

(3) Recognizes Gender: Moderate Gender Culture

Unlike nearby Japan, which ranks highest on masculinity (at 95), South Korea is a moderately feminine culture, at least when it was originally studied. This means that social gender roles are not as distinct. However, it must be stated that the most influential and powerful positions in South Korea have traditionally been given to men, and South Korea still retains a lot of masculine culture, which gravitates toward competition, long hours, professional leadership, and material success.

(4) Dislikes Ambiguity: Very High Uncertainty Avoidance

South Korea ranks extremely high on uncertainty avoidance. You will notice that it is roughly twice as high as the US. Although there are, of course, exceptions, Korean society avoids change and uncertainty. They will always move toward closure and certainty rather than open-endedness and unknown situations. They may even feel threatened or act impulsively under unclear situations or ambiguous circumstances.

(5) Looks Ahead: Very High Long-term Orientation

You will, no doubt, have noticed that South Korea scored a 100 on the long-term orientation index. This is the highest of any country, and it helps travelers understand that Korea looks toward the future and is not as concerned about the present. Koreans are not interested in quick results or in making leisure time paramount in their lives. Koreans like to order relationships by status, they are relentless and persistent, and they are also deeply aware of how their life decisions today could bring shame on their ancestors— long away deceased—or descendants.

(6) Delays Gratification: High Restraint

American culture is more than twice as indulgent as South Korean society is. Korea's ability to delay gratification is connected to the government's ability to regulate behavior, apply strict social norms, and generally maintain a culture of hard work and even self-sacrifice for the sake of family, friends, and the greater society. When it comes to work and play, work definitely has the upper hand.

(7) Communicates Indirectly: High Context

South Korea is a culture that speaks more indirectly than directly. While Americans, for instance, are known for their directness, Koreans communicate indirectly, so paying attention to tone and body language is just as important as the explicit words spoken.

(8) Works Tirelessly: High Doing Society

As a society, South Korea has some of the longest school and work hours of any nation on the planet. There is a strong undercurrent of success, hard work, and good pay. From an early age, parents will sacrifice themselves in the hopes that their child will become a wealthy doctor or successful professional. When I lived in South Korea, I was shocked at students who were in school all day, just to have that followed by night school (even for young children), and working professionals routinely worked more than 15 hours a day.

Many More Cultural Elements

To be sure, as discussed in the chapter before, there are a lot more than eight elements of culture apparent in any given society. Cultures can differ radically depending on their views toward race and ethnicity, sexuality, religion, the environment, and honor and shame. Still, the eight cultural dimensions discussed in this chapter will enable you to unlock a culture with confidence and know how to navigate it successfully and intelligently when in-country.

I also recognize that is easy to become overwhelmed when thinking about how to follow protocols in different cultures. I've traveled around the world, and I have many personal stories of cultural misunderstanding, including in Confucianist Asian regions like China, Hong Kong, Singapore, and Japan. In each of these countries, I can think of specific instances where I missed a cultural norm or did not follow the standard protocol for something.

Conclusion

Two things are helpful to keep in mind. First, most everyone you encounter will know that you are not a local. So, they will understand if we are unable to observe all the cultural norms or if you miss context clues that natives instantly recognize. Second, traveling to new contexts is all about learning, and learning is oftentimes about making mistakes (and sometimes downright embarrassing yourself). It is given and assumed that we will commit some cultural fouls when in a foreign context, but what is most important is our desire to understand and respect the local culture as much as possible. As author David Livermore writes, growing in cultural intelligence is about "reaching across the chasm of cultural difference in ways that are loving and respectful."[1]

Reflection Questions

1. How high do you think your CQ is right now? How about your EQ?

2. Are there any ways you markedly differ from the "typical" American?

3. Who is the first person you normally greet at a work or social function? How might it be different in a Confucian-based society?

4. How would you fare in a high work ethic society like Korea?

---

1 David Livermore, *Cultural Intelligence: Improving Your CQ to Engage Our Multicultural World* (Grand Rapids, MI: Baker, 2009), 17.

5. Does making mistakes and learning a foreign culture seem like fun or like a difficult challenge? How can you orient your mind in such a way that you act more like a child who rapidly learns and isn't afraid of mild social consequences?

CHAPTER 12
CULTURE SHOCK

Complaining in Cambodia

We were in Phenom Penh, the capital of Cambodia that is bristling with life and energy. Almost from the start, I could notice a couple of people from our group who were becoming extremely disoriented and increasingly irritable. They were constantly complaining about the heat and humidity, the never-ending noise in the city, the exotic food we ate, and the trash lining most of the streets. Although we were eventually able to help them process what they were experiencing and encourage them to adopt a new mindset, it was not an easy task.

What Culture Shock Is

Coined in the middle of the twentieth century, "culture shock" is a well-known phenomenon that can occur to travelers in a foreign country. Sometimes also referred to as "culture stress," it is most prevalent among those who stay overseas for a substantive period of time—over the course of several months or more. Culture shock can be deeply disorienting, occurring when a person is confronted with a vastly different way of life, unfamiliar customs and beliefs, and new foods, routines, and living habits. It often proceeds in fairly predictable stages until the traveler ultimately adapts to the new culture, only to possibly resurface when that person returns back to his or her own home culture.

For the most part, however, those who spend only a few days or one or two weeks traveling overseas—especially if part of a group or if on vacation—will not experience culture shock, or at least not with great intensity. Still, disorientation can occur, and I have witnessed travelers experience culture shock in a noticeably short amount of time. If this happens to you, recognize that it is normal and that your disorientation, confusion, and sense of imbalance will subside. Eventually, you will either transition into your new environment or, if you do not, it will not be too long before you return to your own culture.

5 Stages of Culture Shock

As mentioned above, many people (though certainly not all) who experience culture shock progress along a fairly predictable set of stages. A twentieth-century academic named Kalervo Øberg argued that travelers experienced four general stages of culture shock, and, later, Peter Adler developed and added a fifth stage. My findings confirm much of what they discovered, though I slightly modify the stages as follows: (1) anticipation, (2) awareness, (3) angst, (4) adjustment, and (5) acceptance. Øberg contended that most every traveler will experience these realities if traveling long enough, though not with the same intensity or at the same time.

(1) Anticipation

The first phase of culture shock is excitement and anticipation. Many travelers are elated—after weeks or months of long-awaited anticipation—to finally be in a new setting, and they are thrilled to be eating exciting food, meeting interesting people, and receiving unique opportunities. They feel like they are in a dream, or what Øberg called the "honeymoon" phase.

(2) Awareness

After one's initial excitement subsides, people begin to see the chasm separating their "normal" routine back home from their "abnormal" one in a new country. Things unnoticed a few days or weeks before are becoming increasingly apparent. This awareness eventually takes someone to the third stage: angst.

(3) Angst

Disorientation or shock follows the awareness that things are not "normal." A sort of anxiety, panic, criticism, aggressiveness, or frustration may result from the loss of those things most familiar and comforting to a traveler: their favorite foods, their beloved TV shows, their ability to speak and understand the language, sleeping habits, their friends back home, and so on. This crisis or "shock" can last a few days, weeks, or months depending on the person and the exact situation.

Figure 12.1 Culture Shock Is Real. When Traveling Overseas, Do Not Be Surprised If You Experience It. It Is Normal.

(4) Adjustment

This stage occurs when a person begins to find ways to positively adjust to one's new surroundings. It is not immediate, and it takes time and intentionality to begin acculturating to the host environment. This can be accomplished by making changes to your diet, learning new words or phrases in the local language, making friends, and rearranging your schedule.

(5) Acceptance

Finally, there is an eventual acceptance of the host culture. The traveler pushes through the challenges faced when traveling to a new country, makes necessary adjustments, and accepts the present realities with good cheer.

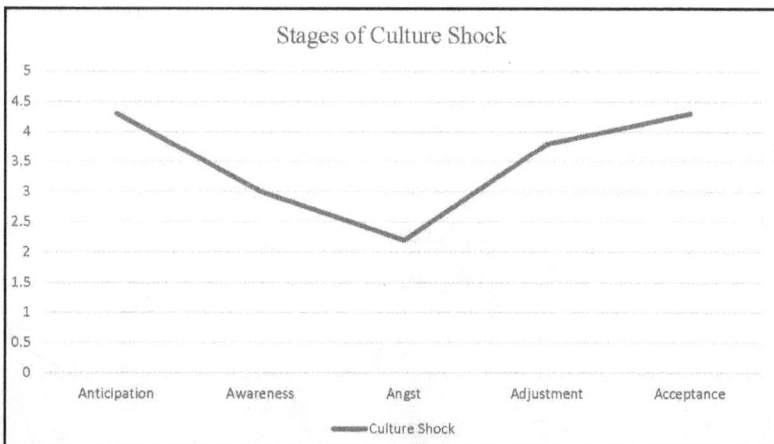

Stages of Culture Shock

Anticipation Awareness Angst Adjustment Acceptance

Culture Shock

Reverse Culture Shock

It is also important to recognize that the stages of culture shock do not necessarily end once all the stages are encountered. Depending on the length of time a person spends abroad, the specific context in which he or she is living, and the nature of their own personality, they could experience the different stages again, particularly when returning home. This phenomenon, called "reverse culture shock," can occur when a traveler— typically after living months or more abroad—can be "shocked" from their own culture. If this happens, as I stated above, rest assured that you are not alone and this is not unusual or a cause of concern: The disconnect you are experiencing will subside, and you will find balance and will learn how to integrate into your home culture.

How to Mitigate Culture Shock

It should be noted that Øberg and Adler's initial research and findings have been modified by later scholars, so what you encounter in a foreign culture may or may not find an exact parallel. And to be sure, not everyone starts an international trip with anticipation and excitement. On the contrary, some travelers are downright nervous or worried about their journey, which anxiety only increases when they arrive. Still, the stages discussed provide a helpful guide to this common phenomenon, and below are some ways to mitigate culture shock if encountered.

- Do not fight against the cultural differences you are experiencing. They are real.

- Focus only on what you can control. Do not waste time obsessing over things you have no power to change.

- Have an open mind and stay positive. Try new foods, adopt new routines, and make new friends.

- Find ways to exercise, practice the local language, and try to think like an insider.

- Get lots of sunlight, preferably earlier in the morning.

- Become more outward focused. Extroverts tend to do better with culture shock than introverts, partly because they externalize their thoughts and process them quicker and with more effectiveness. However, introverts can and should journal their thoughts.

- Avoid extreme, either-or positions. For instance, do not consider cultural differences a matter of "right" and "wrong" or "smart" and "stupid." The situation is more complex than that.

- Keep in touch with friends and loved ones back home. Have a daily video chat, text, call, and make posts about your experiences. There is nothing like the sound of a loved one's voice to soothe the chaos caused by unfamiliar experiences.

- Have a sense of humor and do not forget to laugh. Find something amusing every day that makes you chuckle, even if that means laughing at yourself.

Conclusion

As previously mentioned, the stages of culture shock are usually encountered among those who spend a considerable amount of time in a new culture—typically months or more. When leading short overseas trips (of one to two weeks), I rarely witness travelers experience all stages of culture shock; or, if so, it is in an abbreviated form, beginning with excitement, then presenting mild symptoms of feeling disconnected or being critical, followed by acceptance. At the same time, the stages discussed have been very influential, and it is comforting to know that what you may experience overseas is not unusual but shared by countless other travelers.

Reflection Questions

1. What might the difference be between a bad day and culture shock? How would you know it when you see it?

2. Would it be of any benefit to not only dream about the fun you will have on a trip but also prepare mentally for stressful events that occur?

3. What ways can a person renormalize in a foreign environment?

4. Which tip resonated with you the most concerning mitigating culture shock?

5. If you experience culture shock on a high level, would you cut your trip short or would you persevere? What would your metaphorical red line in the sand be? It is worth considering before you embark.

CHAPTER 13
JET LAG

Leaving Japan

We had just left Japan and were headed to Hawaii. We had left Asia at night and arrived in the island paradise in the morning. Upon exiting the airport and feeling the warm heat of tropical living, we got a second wind as we arrived in our hotel in Honolulu. After we unpacked our bags, we walked to the beach (Waikiki is still the best beach I've ever visited) and had a bite to eat before returning to our room around noon for a "very short" nap. About five hours later, we all awoke only to discover that it was dark outside, and we were as groggy as groggy can be. Now wide awake, we knew that we were in for a very long night.

Collision Course

Everyone who's traveled overseas knows about jet lag. It's the inevitable collision that takes place between your circadian rhythm and your new time zone. The farther you travel, the bloodier the battle. And the older you get, the more susceptible you become.

Being Beat Up in Slow Motion

For me, jet lag is hardest when flying to and from the Asia-Pacific region. While I'm crossing time zone after time zone from the comfort of my airline seat, my body is taking a toll. Each new time zone traversed is a delayed punch to the head and jab to the gut. It's like being beat up in slow motion.

Jet Lag "Disorder"

Medical experts call this phenomenon a "disorder"—and

understandably so. Jet leg is all about your body, spirit, and mind being temporarily out of sorts. It's when your body becomes fatigued, your spirit gets grumpy, and your mind turns mushy. Although these symptoms aren't life-threatening, they can be trip-deflating.

I Paid All This Money to Just Feel Like This?

For most international travelers, every hour counts. They want to make the most of their trip, recognizing that they have tight itineraries to follow, numerous sites to visit, and several trains to catch. They don't have time to feel nauseous, to lose a day to sleep, or to be grouchy.

RESET: Five Ways to Fight Jet Lag

Fortunately, there are remedies to jet lag—including ones that don't require prescription medication or expensive treatments. When I lead groups overseas, I recommend 5 tried-and true ways to fight jet lag. I arrange these steps into a memorable acronym spelling the word "reset," which is exactly what you have to do when traveling overseas.

STEP 1: Redirect

We begin our trip by redirecting. And by "redirect," I'm referring to everything: mentally adjusting our expectations, bodily orienting to our new time zone, and emotionally preparing for a foreign culture. And this starts on the plane—if not days before. Don't wait until you pass through customs before you adopt a new mindset.

This first step is all about mind over matter. You have to motivate your mind to get with the program. It's about assertiveness, disposition, and determination. Because you will soon be on somebody else's cultural turf, your expectations about what is normal, what is fair, and what is comfortable have to be curbed. You will have to start playing by other people's rules, and the first step is recognition of this new reality.

While on the plane, take an honest self-assessment. Are you ready to travel? Is there anything mentally hindering you? Jot down any thoughts that come to mind.

Next comes the body. Begin orienting to your new time zone and eating and drinking patterns while in the air—or, if you are really on your game, a couple of days before your trip. And when on the plane, take a nap or eat your food when you think you will be doing these things in your new time zone.

STEP 2: Exercise

After your mind has made the conscious decision to embrace what is coming, and you have begun—even if modestly— adjusting to a new mental timetable, your body has to fall in stride. You need to exercise. And I am not talking about running a marathon. What I mean is that your body needs to become—and remain—active. While you were enjoying hour after hour of movies on the plane, your body was stagnating in a pool of inactivity.

You now need to restart it by getting your blood pumping, your oxygen flowing, and your legs moving. The lower circulation of oxygen and lower amount of activity you experienced on the plane has to be countered, and one of the best ways to do so is by taking a brisk walk outdoors. The sunnier your walk, the better, since the Sun will help your synchronization to a new circadian rhythm. In fact, getting as much sunlight as possible is crucial, especially in the mornings.

Can't take a walk outside? Then take the stairs rather than escalators at the airport, do some jumping jacks in your hotel room, or take a bicycle tour of the town you're visiting. Just get active—and find time every day to burn some calories. As I alluded to above, always try to do this outside in the sunlight, but do the best you can.

Figure 13.1 Jet Leg Is More Common Than You Think When Traveling Overseas. Follow These 5 Steps to Overcome It.

STEP 3: Socialize

How many times have you fallen asleep while in a conversation with someone? Probably not too often. Socializing actually provides lots of benefits. To begin with, it spurs the production of oxytocin, a hormone that elevates your mood. In this way, socializing makes you feel good. Next, talking with someone else will help keep you alert, especially if it's someone you don't know well, or not at all. There's nothing ruder than falling asleep when someone else is trying to talk with you. Here, peer pressure is a good thing.

Another benefit of socializing is the motivation and accountability that comes with it. The other person can keep you from doing what you desperately want to do—snuggling up in a corner by yourself and dozing off. But don't be that guy or gal all alone snoring in the background.

When I lead groups that cross several time zones, I sometimes pair up everyone with a sleep accountability partner.

"No sleep until at least 9:00 PM," I insist. "Whatever you do, make sure your partner doesn't fall asleep until then."

STEP 4: Eat and Drink

Dehydration begins the moment you arrive at the airport. Before you can even enter your terminal, you have to pass through security—and that means emptying your bags of all liquids. Once you enter your terminal and gate, it's tempting to turn your nose up at a bottle of water selling for $4, so you may skip it altogether. Or, worse, you head for an airport bar and fill up on beer, which will dehydrate you even more. Hours later, when you're on the plane, you may understandably forego liquids to avoid having to use a tiny restroom or disrupting the person seated next to you; nevertheless, drink as much water as possible.

When you arrive in-country, buy a bottle of water at the airport—even if overpriced—and down it on the spot. Your body is dehydrated, after all, and the extra couple of dollars for the bottle is well worth the cost. Next, you will want to adopt a new eating pattern, one that kickstarts a new circadian rhythm. While eating, but sure to keep a steady stream of water coming your way for the first couple of days, because drinking water covers a multitude of travel ailments.

STEP 5: Turn In

Notice that I didn't write "take a nap." When I once led a group to Singapore, the first thing the travelers wanted to do was go to the hotel and take a nap. That's understandable. We were all exhausted, and sleep was beckoning to us like a bakery store after a month with no sweets.

But it's best to avoid naps, especially the first couple of days. I have found that if I can achieve an entire night of sleep the first two nights of arriving overseas, my adjustment goes much smoother.

I recognize that we are all different—and some people simply have to take a nap—but the goal is to achieve the highest quality of nighttime (not daytime) sleep possible the first two days. In general, you want to avoid anything that hinders sleep: alcohol, caffeine, a heavy meal, bright light, or any work-related items. In turn, you want to employ anything that enhances sleep: ear plugs, sleep mask, background noise, darkness, or a comfortable room temperature.

What about sleep aids? I do recommend them—if they help you fall *and* remain asleep. You have 3 major options: (1) prescription medication, such as Ambien or Lunesta, (2) over-the-counter pills that contain diphenhydramine or doxylamine, such as Benadryl or Tylenol PM, and (3) melatonin, a natural hormone that controls your sleep and wake cycles. There are, of course, many variations, and you will want to consult your personal physician to find what is right for you.

Conclusion

In summary, let's review our ways to fight jet lag disorder by resetting your mental and bodily time clock: (1) redirect, (2) exercise, (3) socialize, (4) eat and drink, and (5) turn in. After traveling overseas for more than two decades, I have found this combination of strategies to be the best possible way to keep my mind, body, and spirit in good health so that I can maximize my travel experience.

Reflection Questions

1. In the past when you travel has anything mentally hindered you from traveling with a healthy mindset?

2. What kind of exercise would fit your situation best for kickstarting your body after a long flight?

3. Speaking of socializing, what would you say to a person either on the plane or officially in your group as you try to stay awake? Just as importantly, what would you not say?

4. What stops people from drinking water while traveling? Based on the Eat and Drink Section, when should you drink a bottle of water?

5. What enhances or detracts from sleep? Have these same things helped or hindered you in your own residence?

CHAPTER 14
RELEASING CONTROL

Demanding in Malaysia

We were two weeks into a trip to Southeast Asia, and one of our travelers was still holding tight to wanting everything done her way. While eating with others, she corrected everyone for not using their forks and knives the "proper" way (even though, ironically, most of the people were trying to learn how to use chopsticks instead of Western utensils). When entering new hotels, she ordered the staff to take her luggage upstairs and unpack it for her, while everyone else was perfectly content to carry their own bags and put their clothes in drawers themselves. Oftentimes, this meant she arrived late to meals since she liked to supervise the staff where to put things, and she thought it rude of us when we proceeded to eat before she arrived. Finally, no matter what form of transportation we used—whether taxi, public bus, or rickshaw—she criticized it. "When I travel," she informed me after almost every ride, "I use only private transportation. This is below me." By the time we arrived in Malaysia, several other travelers were greatly agitated. I, along with another travel leader, tried to talk with her to understand things from her perspective— she apparently had grown up in luxury and only traveled in five-star accommodations—but all she did was air a long laundry list of grievances against our trip and against me as one of the leaders. At the end of our short meeting, she declared, "I expected better."

The Traveler's Prayer

American theologian Reinhold Niebuhr wrote one of the most famous English-speaking prayers in the early twentieth century: "God, grant me the serenity to accept things I cannot change, courage to change the things I can, and wisdom to know the difference."

This is a powerful prayer, used and popularized by Alcoholics Anonymous (AA) and other recovery groups to help bring order, wholeness, and peace to emotional and spiritual brokenness. You have probably heard it before and perhaps even prayed it, even without knowing where it came from. Over time, it has come to be titled "the Serenity Prayer," and understandably so. It appeals to serenity in the face of what may seem like hopeless odds. Nonetheless, I prefer to call it "the Traveler's Prayer." That's because it gets to the heart of not only an important life lesson, but also a hallmark feature of international travel: You cannot control your environment, and the sooner you come to peace (or "serenity") with that, the better for you and for everyone you encounter when traveling. Unfortunately, this is easier said than done. Like countless travelers before her, the traveler I mentioned above never released control during her trip, and that refusal to let go affected every aspect of her experience—as well as that of everyone traveling with her.

Applying the Traveler's Prayer to Your Trip

Let's briefly unpack the Traveler's Prayer, starting with the first line: "God, grant me the serenity to accept things I cannot change." This line is all about control. According to the Bible, we all come to the end of our rope eventually. We all have to come to terms with the fact that many things are simply out of our control, and they always will be. We have domain over very little. We are not God. When applied to travel, this speaks for itself: You have to let go of control and, in its place, you need to ask for the kind of transformative peace that causes you to admit, accept, and apply this to everyday situations.

The next line states, "Courage to change the things I can." As a traveler, you cannot control the weather, the foreign culture, or your fellow travelers. But you can control one thing: your attitude. You can control how you respond to adversity. By putting into practice the content discussed in this book, you can begin controlling your responses to situations out of your control, and even doing so with poise and composure. It most certainly takes courage to accomplish this, since we are often our worst enemies, but you have at your disposal support from many sources: friends, fellow travelers, family, faith, and inner fortitude.

Finally, there is the last line of the prayer: "And wisdom to know the difference." There are things we can change, and there are things we can't. When traveling with groups, I sometimes ask them at the end of the day: "What happened that you could have changed today, and what happened that you could not?" This is a profitable exercise. I recommend asking yourself this question every time you encounter a setback, challenge, or frustration. If it turns out you are able to change something, then change it. But if not, then don't dwell on it. Don't assume the authority that God alone possesses. It makes no sense to grieve over what you can't change. Perhaps, for instance, you were planning on taking a train from Barcelona to Madrid. However, when you arrived to purchase your ticket, you were too late, and the train already left. Can you change this situation? Of course not, the train has left. As such, let your frustration leave with it. But does that mean that you are powerless now? Not at all. You still have lots of options: You could wait for the next train, you could hire a taxi or Uber, or you could take a flight.

As a traveler, always keep this prayer at the tip of your tongue. And use it whenever you find yourself in a difficult situation. Accept the things beyond your control but change the things you can.

The 7 Traveling Virtues: Living between Flexibility and Ambiguity

Over the course of two decades of leading international trips, I have concluded that there are seven traits that are important for those who travel. Others are certainly free to disagree, and they may have their own unique list of traits, but I have seen first-hand how the virtues discussed in this chapter greatly enhance people's travel experiences, not only giving them categories to grow into but also helping them fight certain tendencies that we all have as human beings. Both the number seven as well as the concept of virtue stretches deep into the classical world. As you may know, the number seven symbolizes completeness or wholeness in many ancient cultures, occurring hundreds of times in the Bible. Meanwhile, a virtue is a trait deemed excellent or morally worthy, and there are several virtues that are commonly praised in the Christian tradition (charity, faith, fortitude, hope, justice, prudence, and temperance).

Virtually all civilizations of the past, as well as those of the present, laud certain virtues to be morally better than others and worthy of our attention. Below, I list my set of seven travel virtues within the context of releasing control. In order to acquire one of the seven virtues, you will need to let go of something standing in its way: plans, preferences, power, circumstances, offenses, assumptions, and certainty. In the context of travel, these are what I call "the Seven Traveling Vices" (not to be confused with the Seven Vices of the Christian life, though there is some overlap). Once you release these vices and acquire their contrasting virtues, you will be well on your way toward traveling with a better frame of mind and a greater potential to meet and overcome any challenge.

(1) Acquire Flexibility: Release Control of Your Plans

"But," one of my travelers protested, "our itinerary says we are supposed to be having lunch at *this* restaurant in the Old City." He then pointed to the name of the restaurant on the paper as if the case were closed. "That's true," I replied, as patiently as I could. "That *was* the plan. But as I said to everyone a moment

113

ago, we just learned that someone was stabbed a block from the restaurant, so the whole area is closed off. Not even locals can get in, much less a group of tourists. Trust me—the restaurant we are going to is really good and offers a great alternative. But we just can't push past a police barricade or wait several hours before everything clears up. We need to eat now, and this is our best option."

If I could inject international travelers with just one virtue, it would be flexibility. It is that important. Imagine yourself riding a motorcycle on a winding road that is swirling up a mountain while pebbles, rocks, and boulders are slowly tumbling down the mountain all around you. If you stay in the same lane without swerving around the impediments coming your way— under the bullheaded mindset that you will stay the course since that is what you had planned—you will eventually be knocked off your motorcycle, and you might also injure others. But if you simply adjust your course, you will make it to the top of the mountain without crashing or hurting anyone—including yourself.

As a traveler, you are going to have to curve around the obstacles thrown your way every single day. These obstacles could come in the form of a police barricade (as in the example above), a flat tire, or a lost passport, but staying flexible is what will keep your spirits up when the unexpected tries to knock you down. Every single day, you need to release control over your plans, itineraries, and schedules. Perhaps, like a boomerang, everything you release will come back to you without a hitch— and if that's the case, good for you and congratulations. But when the opposite happens—and believe me, it will happen if you travel enough—you will then be in a much better frame of mind to handle whatever comes your way.

Game Plan: When traveling overseas, move from intractability to flexibility. Intractability is all about persisting in your own way even though it is shown to be outdated, off course, or unrealistic. Flexibility is all about changing your course when you realize you need to pivot.

(2) Acquire Adaptability: Release Control of Preferences

The moment I walked into my room in Finland, I knew some travelers were going to be upset. First, not only were the "double beds" that I requested actually "singles," but, second, they were positioned right next to each other like interlocking chairs, and the room left no extra space to separate them. Every traveler and his or her roommate was going to get to know each other very quickly since they would be sleeping just inches apart. It made little difference that I had previously arranged for double beds that were separate from each other. There were no other rooms available—and, besides, they all had the same configuration—so we were going to have to alter our expectations and make the best of the situation.

Savvy travelers are those who adapt well to their new surroundings. For some, this is intuitive and does not require any great effort. It is simply recognizing that a foreign culture is like visiting a chiropractor—it requires adjustments. For many others, however, it is a skill that has to be cultivated. Or worse, a gift that some have never been given. It is a truism that many Americans possess high standards and reject the notion of being out of their comfort zones. They love their routines. They are used to sleeping in King-sized beds on ergonomically supported foam cushions. They are used to sipping on Diet Sodas with piles of ice and getting refills free of charge. And they are used to entering a store and commanding immediate service with a smile and a life-time guarantee.

Believe me, I get it. I enjoy being comfortable as much as the next person. But preferences are a relative thing. What we grow accustomed to in one culture cannot be easily adapted to another, so more often than not, you are the one who will have to do the adapting if you want to travel without constantly getting annoyed, becoming judgmental, or raining on somebody's parade. When traveling, we are going to have to release control over many of our preferences. This won't be easy, but the reward is great.

Game Plan: When traveling overseas, move from preference to adaptability. Preference is all about doing things exactly the way you want them done. Adaptability is all about assessing your new situation, recognizing how you need to readjust, and then accommodating to your new circumstances with good cheer.

(3) Acquire Humility: Release Control of Power

I once led a CEO of a Fortune-500 company to Central America. Back home, this man commanded a yearly salary in the millions, he oversaw thousands of employees, and he traveled around town in a limousine with a chauffeur. He was used to charting his own course and doing everything his way on his terms. On a mission trip to Honduras, however, he was helpless. He couldn't speak a lick of Spanish, he was sensitive to heat and humidity, causing him to feel ill for most of the trip, and he couldn't even hammer in a straight line—which was a mounting problem given that we were there to help build houses for those who had lost their homes during a recent landslide. Nevertheless, this did not stop him from walking around the work site and constantly telling everyone—including the locals supervising us—how to measure wood, how to paint, and how to hammer. But whenever anyone tried to help him with something, he refused, saying things like, "I have an MBA from Harvard, I think I can hammer without your assistance." Perhaps due to his commanding position back home, he was unable to accept help or admit that he couldn't do something.

When we are on our own turf, it's fairly easy to be self-reliant, self-sufficient, and self-governing. After all, we speak the language fluently, we know where everything is located—from supermarkets to hospitals to train stations—and we can get whatever we need whenever we need it. And for those who are adults, we may own homes, supervise employees, and have more degrees than a thermometer. In short, we are capable, confident, and competent—thank you very much. But that's at home. Overseas is a different story. When abroad, we most likely cannot speak the language, we do not know where anything is located or even exactly how to get there, and all of our normal go-to advice, solutions, and responses offer little guidance, if any at all. All of our training in school and work can seem pointless in the face of a foreign culture that follows a different standard of measure. In such a situation, we seem to yield extraordinarily little power and influence.

Traveling overseas provides an unparalleled opportunity to practice humility, which is the state of remaining low to the ground, not holding your head up high under the presumption that you are entitled or know more than you think you know. To put it plainly, you probably do not know more about your foreign destination than your experienced tour leader, your native taxi driver, or your seasoned travel agency. Nor are you above them. International travel offers people who love to be in charge a sabbath of rest, an opportunity to trust others in ways that they may resist back home. It also offers a wonderful leveling field, where we realize that we are not the center of the universe.

But make no mistake: If you refuse to depend on others and recognize and value them as equals while overseas, you will most likely encounter repeated challenges, make countless mistakes, and annoy or anger those with whom you are traveling. Nobody likes a know-it-all, especially one who actually knows next-to-nothing of their surroundings. In this instance, humility is the best course of action. Release control of power and of being in charge and begin leaning on others and recognizing what they have to offer.

Game Plan: When traveling overseas, move from power to humility. Power is all about you being in charge of everything and assuming that you know best in every situation. Humility is all about you admitting that others, particularly those who are locals or travel experts, can better assess their own environment and that you need to listen to and learn from them.

(4) Acquire Tenacity: Release Control of Circumstances

It was the second day in Stockholm, Sweden, and one of our travelers was having a moment of weakness. Every situation we encountered that day threw him off course. First was the weather. It was cold, windy, and rainy. Next was lunch. He was already sick of eating seafood dishes that he couldn't pronounce. And last was our schedule for the day. On paper, taking a half-day bike ride through the city center sounded like a blast. But apparently, he had assumed—how, I know not— that Scandinavian weather was akin to a Mediterranean climate. Sensing his unease, I tried to reassure him. "Hey, nothing to worry about," I said. "Look around you. Everybody here rides their bikes in the rain. It's normal. Zip up your raincoat and let's have a good time." I then pointed to all the dozens of locals around us riding their bikes in the pouring rain, almost oblivious to the fact that it wasn't sunny and warm.

Figure 14.1 When Overseas, Things Can Happen Outside of Our Control. When This Occurs, Acquire Tenacity.

Travel is never perfect. When the going gets tough, however, the tough get tenacity. And tenacity—otherwise called endurance, grit, or determination—is one of the most powerful forces we can tap into as humans. It's what fuels professional athletes when their energy is depleted, it's what motivates students who are sleepy to study for two more hours for a big test the morning, and it's what drives parents to earn a side job to help pay for their kid's braces.

You are going to encounter setbacks almost every day when overseas. Release control of them. And instead of becoming angry, getting disappointed, or feeling depressed when these setbacks strike, dig your heels in and face these setbacks head-on. Most of these obstacles will be beyond your control, anyway, so there is no reason to hold on to them. But you can still persevere. When it rains, put on your raincoat, and pull out your umbrella; when you get a headache right before a hike, take some Tylenol, eat a snack, and push through; and when you are served a meal that you do not like, take a gulp of water, remain thankful that you have food, and eat it anyway. But whatever you do, don't quit or give up just because it's difficult. Keep on going.

Game Plan: When traveling overseas, move from being overcome by setbacks to tenacity. Setbacks are all about challenges you face that have the potential of wrecking your plans. Tenacity is all about persevering and enduring, even in the face of hardship. When circumstances that are surmountable try to knock you off course, reach deep into your body and tap into that grit and determination that is going to propel you forward.

(5) Acquire Charity: Release Control of Offenses

It was our second day in Bolivia, and we were now taking an hours-long truck ride from La Paz to Cochabamba. It was not the most comfortable drive, and most of us were in the back of the truck along with our bags. At some point along the way, while crossing a river along a bumpy dirt road, one of our bags fell in. This was more serious than it sounds because the river was deep and there was an interesting species of wildlife living inside it: crocodiles. After we communicated that a bag had fallen in the river, we stopped, and the driver, a Bolivian named Sergio, pulled out a long stick from the back of the truck and began fishing for the bag while we watched in amusement as crocodiles swarmed by. We were all laughing and joking about the situation—until we noticed Tim looking angry and cross, sitting by himself in the back of the truck. "Tim, what's wrong?" we asked, only now realizing the issue: It was Tim's bag in the water. Fortunately, Sergio managed to salvage the bag, but not before it got completely drenched. All of his belongings—two months' worth of clothes and supplies—were soaked. We felt bad for Tim and tried to reassure him that it wasn't anybody's fault; it was just an accident. But Tim never forgave the driver, and he sulked behind his wet bag for the rest of the ride.

While traveling overseas, one thing is certain: You will be offended by someone or something. It could be an accident (as above) that puts you at a disadvantage, it could be a fellow traveler who says something careless or even cruel, or it could be a local custom that insults your sense of decency. But whatever it is, it will be your obligation to release control of the offense and put into practice one of the most important virtues of all: charity.

This word "charity," popularized in the King James Bible, is often used in the context of giving donations or money; this is not what I am talking about. I am referring to the older use of the term, which encompasses "love," "grace," and "sympathy." Traveling overseas is not easy, and getting offended is part of the territory, so you will get lots of practice. Not becoming offended at something while traveling with people overseas is like hiking a volcano and not getting sore feet or blisters; it kind of goes with the territory. However, rather than getting offended at your tour leader, your fellow travelers, something inanimate (like a volcano), or even yourself, try a different tactic: Show grace, mercy, and forgiveness. Give everyone and everything the benefit of the doubt. The sooner you do so, the better you will feel, and the better the experience you will have.

Game Plan: When traveling overseas, move from offense to charity. Offense is all about keeping count of wrongs or getting even. Charity is all about extending love, kindness, sympathy, and forgiving wrongs committed against us.

(6) Acquire Teachability: Release Control of Your Assumptions

We were making our way through Seoul, South Korea, and kept coming across socks with intricate designs. Each pair was different, but they all had elaborate images of animals, people, or places. The concept of images on socks was nothing new, but a person in our group named Liz stated the obvious, "Why go to so much effort with these designs when no one will ever see them? What a waste of money—these socks are dumb." I asked her which of these "dumb" socks she liked the most, and she pointed to the ones with the image of a cat. I said to her, "I have an idea. Why don't you buy a pair and wear them tonight? If you still think they're dumb afterward, I'll give you the cash you paid for them." She raised her eyebrow in confusion, but agreed, and wore the socks that evening.

When our group met and walked to the place where we were having dinner—somebody's home—our hosts warmly greeted us at the door and kindly asked us to remove our shoes before coming in. As we all entered the house with no shoes, I complimented Liz's choice of footwear: "Nice socks," I said. She smiled and told me later, "I'm so glad I bought those socks. The ones I was going to wear have holes and stains on them!" In fact, the next day she bought two more pairs because she liked them so much.

Before You Go Overseas

Everyone travels for different reasons, but if you would like to learn and grow while traveling, you will need to release control of your assumptions. In America, for instance, it is customary to wear shoes in our houses. In Asia, by contrast, shoes are only used outdoors. Indoors, it's either bare feet, feet with socks (preferably with cool designs), or indoor sandals. If you think about, this makes perfect sense. Shoes track in water, mud, and dirt, and they also carry all kinds of microbes like viruses and bacteria—picked up from public bathrooms, subway floors, and highly trafficked sidewalks. By banning these germ-filled items from your home, you are reducing your cleaning bill and eliminating potential carriers of sickness.

According to Wiktionary, an assumption can be defined as "the act of taking for granted, or supposing a thing without proof." On the one hand, assumptions are essential to life; every time I drive a car, for instance, I assume that the brakes work. On the other hand, assumptions can be faulty; for example, I assume my friend is angry with me because he hasn't returned my calls, only to realize later that he didn't call back because he lost his phone.

When it comes to international travel, I am referring to this latter example of assumptions. I am talking about those things we believe to be true just because we assume them to be true. Overseas, assumptions can materialize as prejudice or pride. We may think the culture, language, religion, or laws of a certain country are arbitrary or just plain silly, when, in fact, we learn that they all make perfect sense once perceived or experienced from a different perspective. When you travel, be teachable; open your mind and adopt a spirit of learning. Consider yourself a student and your new environment your teacher.

Game Plan: When traveling overseas, move from assumptions to teachability. Assumptions are all about supposing that you know what is best even when you have no real proof. Teachability is all about recognizing that you do not know all things, and that you have a lot to learn. Just because something is different does not mean that it is dumb, silly, or backwards.

(7) Acquire Ambiguity: Release Control of Certainty

We had recently arrived in Thailand, and I quickly noticed that one of our travelers was having a hard time. He was as dazed and confused as a deer in head lights. Nothing made sense to him. The Thai language was tone-based and so challenging that he couldn't even say the word "thank you" without locals snickering. The traffic was a nightmare, he concluded, with no order, and people doing whatever they wanted. What's more, not even the toilets cooperated with his sense of decency: Half of them were nothing more than holes in the floor (what we call "squatty potties"), and the other half had water that swirled the opposite way when flushed. He felt like he was living in the twilight zone or some bizarre world where everything was flipped upside down.

When a person imagines how he or she can grow in self-understanding, few consider ambiguity something worth mentioning, let alone pursuing. In travel, however, it is absolutely essential.

In fact, along with flexibility, I believe that ambiguity is the single greatest virtue in international travel. As a tour leader, if I have travelers that want to become more flexible and more tolerant of ambiguity, I am ecstatic. How so? According to Merriam-Webster, ambiguity is defined as "the quality or state of having a veiled or uncertain meaning." Ladies and gentlemen, this is the essence of international travel. Being in a foreign culture, after all, is the equivalent of wearing a veil over your eyes, when your vision is always partially obscured, and you never see anything with perfect sight.

In cultural studies, we call this "ambiguity tolerance." The higher the ambiguity tolerance, that is, the higher a person's capacity for not understanding what is going on, the more a person can sustain uncertainty. A person with a low ambiguity tolerance, by contrast, cannot withstand uncertainty and confusion. They need things to be immediately clarified and instantly explained.

When it comes to international travel, the higher the ambiguity tolerance a person has, the more success he or she will achieve. That is because being overseas is the equivalent of only understanding half of what is communicated. You will have to come to terms with the fact that you will never fully understand the language spoken, many customs will be an absolute mystery, and a lot of your interactions with locals will turn out differently than you want. In order to make the most of your experience, release control of certainty. Revel in the mystery of not knowing.

Game Plan: When traveling overseas, move from certainty to ambiguity. Certainty is all about everything following a predetermined order and making perfect sense. Ambiguity is all about the rationale, explanation, or purpose behind almost everything being unclear, incomplete, and unresolved.

Conclusion

In my experience leading international trips, releasing control is one of the most important things we can do. It can literally be the difference between having an amazing trip and having a terrible one. The simple act of letting go is like a personal revolution that can completely transform your attitude—and, as a result, your experience. Sometimes when I have a traveler on one of my groups that I can tell really struggles with control, I advise them to extend their hands with their palms up and mentally imagine releasing whatever it is that they are holding onto. It is almost always one of the themes discussed in this chapter, though it can also be their work commitments back home or a family member that they miss. I also encourage them to journal about their struggles with control, processing them with someone on the trip, and praying for supernatural strength. By putting into practice these exercises—and repeating them as needed—your travel experience is destined for success.

Reflection Questions

1. Were you already familiar with the Traveler's Prayer or one like it? Why do you think it so popular but still underutilized? Why do you think relinquishing control is so hard?

2. Place yourself in a situation like the one describing beds being pushed together. How would you handle it?

3. Think of a time in your life when you exhibited tenacity. How would you tap into that for traveling overseas?

4. Charity often translates into forgiving others or apologizing for a misdeed. Is there any way you can practice this virtue before traveling or even this week by apologizing to someone for a wrong you committed or by forgiving a person against whom you are holding a grudge?

5. After learning the reason behind taking off shoes in many countries, would you consider a ban on shoes in your house? What other foreign customs can you think of that would be worthwhile to incorporate into your own home or lifestyle?

CHAPTER 15
ADJUSTING EXPECTATIONS

Disappointment in Costa Rica

I led my first international trip in the year 2000. Traveling to Costa Rica, I created an itinerary that sought to capture all the splendor this amazing country provides: spectacular beaches, volcano hikes, waterfalls, historic churches, delicious food, and lodging in the jungle. Although we experienced all the beauty Costa Rica has to offer, we also encountered our fair share of setbacks. On the first day, the public bus broke down in the mountains. The driver then packed up his belongings and disembarked, leaving us to walk to the nearest town to hire a taxi. A few days later, someone from our group ran a couple of errands in the nation's capital by himself. Because he was not paying attention to his surroundings, his passport and credit card was stolen. Two days afterward, a traveler got sick, and I ended up taking her to a medical clinic. The next day, while visiting the largest volcano in Costa Rica, someone complained, "This isn't that impressive; I've climbed mountains much bigger." He had always imagined hiking a volcano akin to trekking Mount Everest, so he was upset when facing something much less intimidating.

Great Expectations

Expectations are hard to satisfy and almost impossible to exceed. We have all been disappointed by people who said one thing yet did another and technology that promised better results only to not work when most needed. When it comes to international trips, one of the most disastrous things we can do is expect too much. In my 25 years of leading trips, I have no memory of one that did not encounter at least one bump along the way. Whether it rains on a day we are planning to be outside, a museum we are scheduled to visit is closed for restoration, or there is no Wi-Fi in our hotel, our expectations do not always match reality. When this happens, how will you respond?

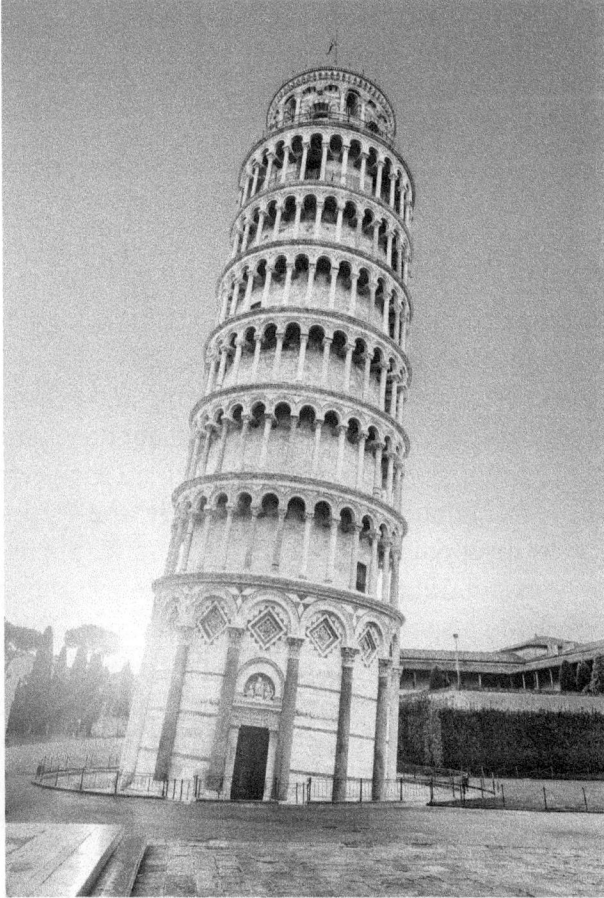

Figure 15.1 Expectation Does Not Always Match Reality. When This Happens, Follow These 4 Steps.

Dealing with Disappointment

Let's be direct here: You *will* be disappointed with something on your trip. Whether it's disappointment at a site, lodging, meal, or person—you will experience the sadness, frustration, or letdown that always accompanies unfulfilled hopes and unrealized desires. But this does not mean that your trip is ruined or that you have to wallow in despair. In this chapter, I will isolate strategies both (a) to help you deal with disappointment when it inevitably comes and (b) to learn how to better synchronize your expectations with reality.

4 Steps When Disappointment Strikes

We will start with how to deal with disappointment. I recommend 4 steps.

(1) Own Your Disappointment

Owning disappointment involves 3 things: (i) acknowledging that we are upset or sad, (ii) naming the reasons why we are (which introverts accomplish by journaling and extroverts by verbally processing), and (iii) sitting with our disappointment for several minutes (or longer depending on the person and scope of the disappointment). One of the least effective ways to deal with disappointment is to suppress it. Suppression, after all, does not offer a real solution to your problem. It is like submerging a sponge in a sink full of water. Eventually the sponge will reemerge and, when it does, it will have soaked up more water than if you had simply squeezed it and placed it on the counter to fully dry. What's more, our brains are not easily tricked. They transmit chemicals into our body based on our reactions to expectations, meaning that you are fighting against your mind and body when you act like nothing is wrong when it actually is. Don't make that mistake.

(2) Let Bygones Be Bygones

When facing disappointment, many people turn to the blame game. On an international trip, the source of blame can be a travel agent, a tour guide, locals, the weather, a travel companion, or even yourself. This blaming can grow inwardly into shame or self-loathing or outwardly into hostility or passive aggressiveness. All options can prove fatal to a trip (let alone a relationship). Forgiving and not assigning blame may be achieved through prayer, introspection, coming to terms with our own shortcomings, clearing our head, releasing control, and sheer will power.

(3) Recalibrate Your Expectations

Now that you have moved on from being angry or assigning blaming, reassess your situation. Perhaps your expectations were way too high and unrealistic. If so, temper them with something more reasonable. Share your thoughts and feelings with fellow travelers or on the phone with someone at home. Gain needed perspective from them. Aim for expectations that are more reflective of real life.

(4) Find Your Inner Joy

This last step is often accomplished through meditation, yoga, worship, private or communal prayer, devotional reading, taking a walk, or doing something you genuinely enjoy. It is when you dump out all the existing water in your bucket and then send it down into your own spiritual and emotional well to recover fresh water that promotes peace, balance, and joy.

5 Ways to Realign Your Expectations

Now that you have dealt with your disappointment, it is important to set yourself up for success in future endeavors by having a better long-term strategy. Below are 5 steps you can take that can help you have a more balanced and sensible expectation for your trip.

(1) Be Realistic

Nothing is perfect. And almost nothing goes perfectly. Even if you are on your honeymoon, an event you may have planned for years, it is almost certain that something will happen that will dampen your mood or make you upset. Unfortunately, even honeymooners can get on each other's nerves, contract food poisoning, or have their ocean-front hotel room downgraded to a view of the parking lot. International travel is just like life—except that it is life overseas. The same highs and lows apply, so do not expect more than you should. Unrealistic expectations will lead to disappointment.

Pro Tip: Take time to reflect on your last couple of trips. How often did you become disappointed, when did your expectations fail to match reality, and what can you learn and apply to your next trip?

(2) Be Surprised

When I go to a new place for the first time, I sometimes intentionally do not search for pictures or videos online ahead of time. After all, who wants to watch a video of someone enjoying endless sun at a famous landmark only for it to be gray and raining when I go? And when I catch myself daydreaming about what it will be like, I try to pinch myself so that my hopes do not fly away like a balloon into unreality.

Pro Tip: Imagine that you are a cup. Never travel to a new destination while full. Be sure to empty some of its contents so that you have room for what is to come.

(3) Be Flexible

If international travel were a board game, it would be called "flexible," and all the players would have multiple skill sets. In my opinion, flexibility is the single greatest quality needed to successfully travel overseas. If you are incapable of flexibility, stay home; if you are short on flexibility, get more; and if you are overflowing with flexibility, be realistic.

Pro Tip: Consider your itinerary to be a "work in progress." In all my trips, I always state that the itinerary is "tentative," even on the day we are scheduled to visit a place or meet with someone.

(4) Be Patient

Patience is worth its weight in gold when traveling. Take your cues from the first leg of your journey: the airport. Being forced to wait in long lines to check your bags, pass through security, and enter your plane offer a helpful reminder from the start: Travel takes patience—and lots of it.

Pro Tip: Practice makes perfect—and patient. The best way to learn patience is to put yourself in situations where patience is required. Go the supermarket before a large storm, visit the mall during the holiday season, or drive in traffic during rush hour. While in these frustrating situations, figure out best how to cope with them.

(5) Be Selfless

It is almost impossible to feel bad for yourself when assisting others and thinking primarily about their welfare and happiness. Think of ways you can support fellow travelers and offer them assistance. When I travel, for example, I am always assessing how people are doing. When they look lost, I give directions; when they want a group photo, I volunteer to take their picture. Helping others is the best antidote to feeling sorry for yourself.

Pro Tip: There is almost always someone in need on your trip: a fellow traveler, another tourist, a local person. Plan every day on helping at least one person in need. I do this in various ways, including bringing an extra bottle of water to give to a person when thirsty, carrying an extra phone charger for the man who forgets his, and helping an older traveler carry her bags when she looks tired.

Conclusion

It is my hope that you have an amazing experience when traveling overseas, but do not be surprised when you become disappointed at a site you had built up too much in your head, at a hotel whose advertised pictures defy reality, and at travel agencies whose guaranteed list of inclusions include far less than anticipated. When this happens, practice the steps outlined above, and keep a journal so that you can improve.

Reflection Questions

1. What are you most looking forward to on your trip? Are your expectations realistic?

2. If a difficult or unexpected situation arises, what is your default temperament? If you become angry or sad, how will you respond? And how will this affect others?

3. What are some practical ways you can embody patience and kindness while on the trip?

4. What steps can you be taking now in order to cultivate flexibility?

5. If you find yourself disappointed on the trip, who or what can you turn to for help?

CHAPTER 16
CONFLICT RESOLUTION

Not Happy in Hungary

We were a few days into a trip to Hungary when a couple of the travelers reached a boiling point in their conflict. They were students in the same program, but they didn't see eye to eye. Back home in a classroom setting, their aversion to each other was mitigated by the large number of students in their cohort and by never working together in the same study groups. Although this wasn't the best strategy, it kept the peace. Overseas, however, they encountered a totally different context. They were in each other's presence at mealtimes, on bus trips, at sightseeing visits, and in hotel lobbies. Avoidance was no longer an option; we had to help them resolve their conflict before it got out of hand and began infecting the rest of the travelers.

Conflict is Natural and Normal

Conflict is part of life. Wherever two or more are gathered, conflict will eventually follow. Although this isn't always a bad thing, it certainly *can* be. In fact, conflict can sometimes serve as a catalyst to improve a situation, to push beyond false pleasantries, or to clear the air. The goal is not so much to avoid conflict—a common approach many people take—as it is to manage and adequately resolve it. That's because conflict, though starting off small (as in the case of the example above), can quickly escalate and become destructive.

Traveling Can Bring out the Best...and Worst

This is even more apparent when we take into consideration that travel can bring the best out of some people but the worst in others. Anyone who has traveled overseas can attest that it can be disorienting, exhausting, and unpredictable. And, when coupled with going without sleep for two nights in a row, a sensitive stomach from a questionable meal, or disgust for an off-colored joke from someone in your group, our manners and senses of decency can be severely tested. As such, it's not at all surprising that conflict tends to go hand and glove with international travel.

2 Parts of Conflict: Dealing with It and Evaluating How You Dealt with It

We will divide our discussion into 2 parts: (i) listing 5 ways to deal with an *existing* conflict and (ii) asking yourself 5 questions *after* handling a conflict. Also, please note that the conflicts I am addressing in this chapter do not include abuse, harassment, or violence. These matters are never acceptable and remain a separate discussion altogether.

Figure 16.1 All Groups Experience Some Conflict. When This Happens, Follow These 5 Steps.

During the Ordeal: 5 Ways to Deal with Conflict

In this section, we will isolate 5 common (though not exhaustive) ways to deal with conflict, all of which start with the letter "c": conceal, confront, concede, compromise, and collaborate. These approaches are not ranked in any particular order. However, depending on the exact situation, the parties involved, the severity of the ordeal, and the history of it occurring, some approaches have more merit than others. And because we are focusing on conflict as it pertains to international travel (which is usually short-term or isolated), we will not discuss long-term resolution tactics.

(1) Conceal

Probably the most common way to deal with conflict is to avoid it. Depending on the situation, this is also one of the easiest approaches. If you are traveling with a large group, for instance, you may conceal your conflict with another person by avoiding them or acting like nothing is wrong. In fact, some people are so good at concealing a conflict that the other person does not even realize that he or she is the source of anger, concern, or dislike.

Retreating from an actual or potential conflict situation is almost never a good long-term strategy, but it is sometimes the most effective approach for short-term circumstances. For example, I remember spending two days in Nicaragua with a traveler named Burt (I am "concealing" his real name). I really disliked him. Everything he said and did rubbed me the wrong way, though, to be fair, I do not believe he was mean or malicious. After the first few hours with him, I considered my options (that is, the different approaches listed here), but I ultimately decided to say or do nothing since I knew that we were only going to be part of the same travel group for 24 hours and then I would never see him again. As such, I simply avoided being around him as much as possible and tried to conceal my dislike.

When to Use This Tactic: You may want to consider concealing your conflict with another person when (i) you are outranked or under that person's authority or employment (and especially if that person is punitive), (ii) you need time to think and reflect before responding, or (iii) you will only be with that person for a short amount of time.

(2) Confront

Believe it or not, there are some people who love conflict and rush toward it like lions fighting over a lame gazelle. This is the most aggressive and direct way to handle a conflict. There are different results that can stem from a confrontational approach to conflict. First, it is possible that your conflict is a zero-sum game, where one person wins and the other loses. This represents a more competitive way to address conflict. Second, it is possible that your confrontation may be welcomed, and you eventually find a way to resolve the situation. Third, the confrontation could escalate or backfire. Perhaps you underestimated the person's response, or perhaps you did not consider all the possible consequences. A confrontational approach to conflict tends to work best when both parties are reasonable, direct, less prone to visceral responses, and willing to admit fault.

By way of an example, I remember a trip I had in Germany where a confrontational approach was taken by a couple of the travelers. It was the first day, and everyone was still getting to know each other. There were a couple of guys in particular, some of us noted, who had strong personalities, and you could tell that they were sizing each other up. As we discussed dinner options and could not come to an agreement about where to eat, the conflict that had festered between them over the course of the day flared up and they decided to confront each other then and there. Soon, everyone had forgotten about being hungry, and we had to find a way to keep these guys from getting into a fist fight.

When to Use This Tactic: You may want to consider confronting a conflict when (i) you are in an emergency situation and you need to act quickly, (ii) you or someone in your group is in danger, or (iii) the group is being negatively impacted by a situation because it remains unresolved or unaddressed.

(3) Concede

This approach is akin to smoothing or accommodating to someone else. It can also be about emphasizing areas of agreement rather than areas of disagreement. In the context of traveling, it is often about conceding one's position to the needs of others to maintain harmony and good will.

For part of a tour I led in Egypt, for instance, we had budgeted for travelers to stay in the home of locals for two nights. We had all agreed to this arrangement before the trip began and planned accordingly, but when the day arrived, one of the travelers said that he did not want to stay in a stranger's house, and, instead, he demanded a hotel room for himself. As I tried to press him about this situation, I could tell that he was adamant and increasingly defensive, and so I weighed my options. Ultimately, I conceded to his request and paid for him to have a hotel room by himself for those two nights, along with his breakfast and dinner expenses included at the hotel. This negatively affected our budget, but I thought it better to give him what he wanted rather than see this conflict escalate inside the home of a host who would not know how to respond to the situation. The extra couple of hundred dollars outweighed a conflict that could have jeopardized the safety of our group and hosts.

When to Use This Tactic: You may want to consider conceding a conflict when (i) it is in the best interest of the group, (ii) you may lose more in the long run if you don't accommodate, or (ii) you will not get your way regardless of the outcome.

(4) Compromise

Compromising is about searching for solutions that bring some degree of satisfaction to all parties involved. Stated differently, a compromise is achieved when demands from each party are adopted so each person or party achieves a small victory. Compromise does not work in every situation, and it can sometimes cause more harm than good or even intensify the situation, but it is a valid approach that some people prefer when settling a conflict.

When I was once leading a group in the Czech Republic and Slovakia, for instance, we had two free days scheduled. I had devised a series of options but had not booked anything. While on the trip, I cast a vision for what we could do, which included a jam-packed set of days seeing as much as possible, on the premise that this is the only time the group might ever visit these places, so I wanted to show them as much as possible. It turns out, though, that only half of the group wanted this active itinerary while the rest wanted to choose one spot and spend the whole time there. In the end, I agreed to a compromise. For the first free day, we would visit a variety of locations and keep active from breakfast till dinner, while, for the other day, we would let those who wanted a quieter schedule to plan our day from morning till night, even if that meant we did nothing at all.

When to Use This Tactic: You may want to consider making a compromise when (i) you have a history of getting things your way, (ii) you want to keep things more balanced, or (iii) the outcome of the decision is inconsequential.

(5) Collaborate

Collaboration is probably the healthiest and most equitable approach to managing conflict. However, it is can also be the most time-consuming and most demanding. Of course, collaboration requires a cooperative attitude and open dialogue that, ideally, leads to consensus, commitment, and concord.

Regrettably, though, some people are defiant, territorial, or unwilling to work with others, so it cannot always be achieved. And because collaboration is best to pursue when you have to engage someone for an extended period of time, it is not feasible for short-term trips that may last no more than week or that are so hectic that no time is available for collaboration.

By way of an example, on a trip I once led to Israel, I created a half-day scavenger hunt inside the Old City of Jerusalem. The travelers, directed to work in groups of three, had to collaborate with their team members to complete the scavenger hunt. Because we were about a week into the trip when this day arrived, I had a particularly good sense of how everyone was getting along—and, in some instances, not getting along. There were a few people, in particular, that seemed to be having a mild conflict with each other. From what I could tell, it was not serious, so I decided to put them together for the scavenger hunt, on the assumption that working together and doing something fun might help them resolve their conflict. Although they were not best friends when they returned, the opportunity to collaborate on something they enjoyed allowed them to move beyond their differences and maintain peace for the rest of the trip.

When to Use This Tactic: You may want to consider collaboration when (i) both parties are responsible and open-minded, (ii) both parties involve leaders who have equal rank or responsibility, (iii) you are trying to build camaraderie or unity, or (iv) you have to work with a person long-term.

How, Why, What, Who, and Where: 5 Questions to Ask After Handling Conflict

Now that the conflict has been addressed, it is important to review your handling of it. This is important for many reasons, not least of which is for you to learn from the ordeal and also to be better prepared for the next time you have to deal with conflict.

For, unfortunately, depending on the situation, the conflict may not immediately (or completely) go away, so you will need to establish a game plan for the future. Moreover, by examining how you handled the conflict, you may also surface your go-to response to conflict, which may or may not need to be improved or modified. Below, we will organize our five questions into the most frequent question-words in our language: "how," "why," "what," "who," and "where."

(1) *How* Did I Handle It?

In what way did you respond? Were you defensive, gracious, or fault-finding? Did you say something you regretted or sense feelings that surprised you? What was your visceral reaction? On a scale of one to ten, how would you rank your handling of the conflict?

(2) *Why* Did I Handle It This Way?

Perhaps you are discovering that you tend to deal with conflicts the same way every time. Does your personality lead you to handle disagreements in a certain way? Is there something in your past that directs you to respond a certain way? Is there a way for you to heal any scars that remain from previous battles with conflict?

(3) *What* Caused It?

What was the exact circumstance that caused the conflict? Was it over a person, a situation, or an event? Are you detecting a particular pattern regarding what causes conflict in your life?

(4) *Who* Was Involved?

Are you noticing that you are coming into conflict with the same person, or is it someone different? If you are regularly coming into conflict with different people, perhaps you need to turn inwardly and examine the kinds of personalities that cause you to respond in a certain way? If you are running into conflict with the same person, figure out a responsible way to deal with him or her.

(5) *Where* Can I Improve?

Nobody's perfect, and we all have areas in our lives where we can grow. Although most of us would prefer to never encounter conflict, it can be used as a tool for self-reflection, self-learning, and self-improvement. Go ahead and identify areas of personal weakness. Write them down in a journal and set yourself goals for how to handle conflict better in the future.

Conclusion

I wish I could say that your international travel experience will be nothing but endless smiles, happy encounters, and amazing experiences. And perhaps it will be. However, do not be overly dismayed if you find yourself getting annoyed at another traveler (including at yourself), saying something you regret, doing something you dislike, or getting into an argument with your travel companion. This kind of conflict is bound to happen when others are along for the ride, and it is especially common when people are outside their comfort zones (perhaps for days or weeks at a time), when they are exhausted from jet lag and busy itineraries, or when they get sick or injured. It is all part of the journey, of course, but it is up to you to make the best of it, to learn from your mistakes, and to keep traveling with an open mind and a gracious spirit.

Reflections Questions

1. Can you recall an instance when you were traveling either abroad or in your home country when a severe conflict erupted? How was it resolved?

2. Out of the first two options, conceal and confront, which one are you most prone to?

141

3. Conceding a conflict means suppressing your ego. How can you practice that habit before you travel overseas and likely must do so multiple times in the same trip?

4. Is there a certain personality type that you know from prior experience sets you off? How might you plan for dealing with that kind of personality type?

5. What area of personal weakness do you exhibit when it comes to conflict resolution? How might you tackle that shortcoming?

CHAPTER 17
SOCIAL MEDIA

Selfies in Italy

I was in Rome, Italy, one of the most popular tourist destinations in the world, standing before perhaps the most iconic landmark in the city: the Colosseum. The last time I was there, I did something I don't always do—I ignored my agenda and just decided to observe. What did I see? If you have been there before, you know the scene: bus after bus of tourists, locals dressed up like gladiators posing for pictures (and tips), and vendors selling water, gelato, and selfie-sticks. And quietly behind all of this, there stands an amazing Roman amphitheater built 2,000 years ago. As I watched all of this unfold, I could not help but notice something very curious—but also quite common. I observed tourist after tourist roll out of a taxi or bus, walk within 100 meters of the Colosseum, snap a picture of themselves, and immediately return to their bus or continue on, most likely to another destination where they would presumably do the same thing.

The Year of the Selfie

When I started leading international trips twenty-five years ago, people took photos, but they rarely shot videos, they never obsessed about finding Wi-Fi, and the word *selfie* hadn't been invented. I'm not one for nostalgia, nor of christening excursions *before* the Internet as "the golden age of travel," but selfies and social media can dampen an amazing trip, or at least cultivate bad habits. And I regret to inform you that, tragically, thousands are injured each year as they pose for selfies in exotic places, and hundreds even die.

Go Ahead and Take that Selfie, Just Don't Let It Overtake Your Trip

Before you get the wrong impression, I hasten to add that I believe selfies have their place, and I encourage you to keep on taking them. In fact, I enjoy them as much as anyone else—just not if they come at the expense of the experience I am seeking to cultivate as a traveler. When wielded properly, social media and cell phones are powerful tools that greatly enhance our lives and our journeys. When you are overseas, it is deeply comforting to have a video chat with a loved one, to text a best friend back home, to take a panorama of an incredible site, or to post a new picture on Instagram. And, as much as we may want to leave work or school behind when away, sometimes it's necessary to send an email to a supervisor, client, or teacher.

Social media, after all, has completely changed how we travel. We're now accustomed to being connected to the world on a minute-by-minute basis, and we often close one app just to open another. Facebook, Snapchat, Instagram, TikTok, YouTube, Twitter, WhatsApp, Reddit, Pinterest—the list goes on and on, with a new app born every day.

Don't Sacrifice Quality of Experience for Quantity of Pictures

When used thoughtlessly, however, social media and cell phones snatch us away from our surroundings. It causes us to spend more time online than on-site. Almost unknowingly, the focus of the trip becomes more about posting show-stopping selfies than about being in the moment. The goal shifts from quality of experiences to quantity of pictures.

To be sure, each of us travels for different reasons, but many do so in order to learn about other cultures, to hear people's stories, to be present in historic places, to grow personally or spiritually, and to see the world from a different perspective. As much as social media can enrich these experiences, it can't replace them.

On this point, I speak from experience, having witnessed how groups can fragment and become socially distant as they turn to their phones rather than to each other. There is certainly a time and place for that, but, in terms of group dynamics and fostering unity and comradery when traveling with others, sometimes the best thing you can do is to give your phone a timeout. It will always be there when you return, and the connections you make with your fellow travelers can last a lifetime.

Figure 17.1 Social Media Is Now Completely Integrated into International Travel. Follow Our 7 Guidelines to Use It Well.

7 Guidelines

In order to make the most of your trip, I recommend observing 7 guidelines related to travel, cell phones, and social media. Note that NONE of these recommends abandoning social media or chucking your cell phone over a cliff: Keep your cell phone and stay linked with contacts back home—just be sure to use electronics as tools rather than as masters.

Before You Go Overseas

(1) Be Advised

Some locations that tourists frequent—such as religious spaces, security checks, government buildings, palaces, and museums—frown upon the use of photography or video, and some prohibit the use of cell phones altogether. If in doubt, always ask before taking a picture or video. If the person you ask cannot speak English, use context clues from body language to discern their answer.

(2) Be Understanding

There are always some in the group who do not want their names or faces to appear on social media (for a variety of reasons). It is always best to ask permission before posting a picture or video of someone else. And it goes without saying that it is bad form to post something unflattering of or about someone. Here the golden rule is best: "Do to others as you would have them do to you."

(3) Be Thoughtful

We have probably all encountered tourist groups that lingered too long in crowded spaces, that did not pay heed to others, and that did not observe rules about keeping quiet or refraining from taking pictures. These groups can leave a bad taste in the mouth of locals and other tourists. Don't forget to be respectful of the people and places you visit.

(4) Be Vigilant

Pickpockets are drawn to tourist locations like bears to honey. Be careful that you are not so focused on taking an incredible selfie or posting the perfect online video that you lose sight of your belongings or surroundings. Tourists have items stolen or lost this way every single day, most of which are never recovered.

(5) Be Discerning

Have you ever tried to tell an inside joke to an outsider?

Stories need context to make sense. What we share on the trip with our network back home can be misperceived or misunderstood without sufficient context. Try to anticipate how your pictures or comments will be interpreted back home before posting them. There is nothing more deflating than receiving critical and negative comments about a post you were excited to share due to your audience not understanding the context of your post.

(6) Be Present

Have you ever shared a meal with someone who was constantly texting? It's not an enjoyable experience. It's hard to be fully present when continually posting pictures or videos online, or when focused on your phone. One of the greatest gifts that we can give to others is being present. Consider spending the bulk of your time on your devices when in your room or when alone.

(7) Be Creative

A stunning photo on Instagram or a perfectly worded tweet on Twitter can capture an audience and make a profound point. Think creatively about how you can share a picture, video, or story from your trip in a meaningful way with those in your network. Let your travel experience inspire you!

Conclusion

If you would like to think more about these dynamics in a group setting, I recommend Sherry Turkle's book, *Reclaiming Conversation: The Power of Talk in a Digital Age*. If you would like to explore the world of travel apps, there are new ones created all the time, and I write elsewhere about many of them. What are some of your favorite apps? When using them, think about how they can enhance your travel experience without becoming the emphasis.

Before You Go Overseas

Reflection Questions

1. Do you like taking pictures or selfies? Even if you aren't naturally inclined to media, why do you think it exerts such a strong influence?

2. Have you been around a person who overemphasized technology to the detriment of a being in the moment? Have you ever caught yourself missing the moment because you were on technology?

3. How long do you think a tourist group should linger in the prime position at a popular destination? What would you consider reasonable?

4. Have you ever posted a picture or wrote a comment on a social media outlet only for it be misperceived?

5. How could you create a feedback loop of comments or pictures in a way that keeps you in the moment as a traveler yet keeps those at home inspired and informed?

CHAPTER 18
KNOW YOURSELF

Encountering an ISTJ in Turkey

In the last group I led to Turkey, I met one of the most interesting travelers I had ever traveled with. From the moment I met him at the airport, I could tell that he was an extremely high Senser and a definite ISTJ, according to the Myers-Briggs Type Indicator. Every day, he asked me the most detailed of questions and saw things that I would never see: the color of socks people wore and the items the average person carried in their hands. While we would be taking a bus through downtown Istanbul, he would ask me things like: "That man over there crossing the road with a blue watch and green eyes, where do you think he is going?" I could barely locate the man he was referring to let alone surmise where he might be headed. A few days before our trip ended, he asked if he could talk with me. The next day I took him to get some ice cream and asked what was on his mind. He pulled out a clearly written document with four items that I needed to improve on, which he explained in detail to me with no emotion whatsoever.

Self-Awareness

In many ways, the longest and most arduous trip you will ever take as a traveler is your own journey toward self-awareness. Travel, after all, is nothing if it is not deeply introspective, uncovering who you really are and helping you understand what you really want out of life. Although we primarily travel to distant lands in search of historic sites, cultural experiences, and beautiful landscapes, trips ultimately offer us—if we are willing to listen and learn—a deeper understanding of ourselves. Toward that end, I want to briefly discuss some of the most well-known self-discovery tools available, such as the Myers-Briggs, the Enneagram, and Strengthsfinder. By becoming familiar with these tools, you will be better equipped to understand and even identify how you will experience the world when traveling.

(1) Myers-Briggs

The Myers-Briggs Type Indicator was developed in the twentieth century based on research conducted by the German psychologist Carl Jung. The indicator argues that differences in behavior are not random occurrences but indicate consistent patterns in the way people perceive, judge, understand, and engage the world. The Myers-Briggs helps us uncover motivations, natural preferences, and strengths, as well as areas of growth. It has been commonly used to provide career guidance, and many employers have also found it helpful to understand their employees. The Myers-Briggs Type Indicator does not measure intelligence or ability, and no type is better or worse than another. For more about the Myers-Briggs, I recommend the following websites: myersbriggs.org and 16personalities.com. As for books, consider reading *Gifts Differing* and *The 16 Personality Types*.

I/E, S/N, T/F, J/P

The Myers-Briggs is composed of sixteen distinct personality types that are combined according to eight different preferences: introvert or extrovert, sensory or intuitive, thinking or feeling, and judging or perceiving. After taking a test online, your preferences will be arranged into one of sixteen personality types consisting of four types, which, when arranged, indicate a specific way of perceiving and engaging the world.

Introversion and Extraversion: How You Gain Energy

The primary difference between these two is the source of their energy. **Introverts** gain energy from the inner world, such as ideas and concepts, while extroverts obtain it from the outer world, such as people and things. This generally results in introverts preferring to work independently, having fewer but closer relationships, liking quieter, slower, and more intimate environments, enjoying depth over breadth, and reflecting inwardly before making decisions. **Extroverts**, meanwhile, prefer working in groups and have many friends and acquaintances, choose breadth over depth, tend to say and process their thoughts aloud, and make decisions quicker than introverts.

Sensing and Intuition: How You Acquire Information

These two are generally divided into how a person acquires information. **Sensers** primarily rely on the five senses to acquire information. They have a natural bent toward details, concreteness, data, and the plain and obvious. They are exceptionally good observers. **Intuiters** naturally see the big picture and do not pay attention to the details. They see patterns, possibilities, and themes, and they are more abstract than Sensers. Intuiters see beyond the details and intuit the meanings lying behind them.

Thinking and Feeling: How You Process Decisions

When making a decision, do you imagine how it will make you or another person feel, or do you make it based primarily on the facts? This gets to the heart of the difference between a T and an F. **Thinkers** focus on the logic of a situation and are grounded in practical and reasonable solutions. They like objectivity, order, and evidence. They tend to be brief and direct and do not tend to think with their emotions. **Feelers**, by contrast, put a lot of weight on feelings, emotions, needs, and values. They make decisions with their heart just as much as with their head, recognizing that one's emotions cannot be separated from decision making. They emphasize relationships, empathy, and getting along with others more so than facts and data.

Judging and Perceiving: How You Live Your Life

Let's say it's 3 days before your trip: Have you packed all your bags, cleaned your house, and set all your bills on autopay? If so, you are probably a J, and if you haven't even washed the clothes you will wear on your trip, you likely qualify as a P. **Judgers** love completing tasks, and they are always attempting to bring closure to something: whether immediately responding to an email upon receiving it or packing for a trip well before the departure day arrives. Judgers like structured, planned, and controlled environments. **Perceivers**, by contrast, procrastinate, keep their options open, and enjoy doing many things without necessarily finishing one or any of them. They are more spontaneous, flexible, and disorganized.

The Myers-Briggs and Travel

The following should be considered as you contemplate your types and travel preferences.

Introverts/Extroverts: Introverts prefer quieter and more intimate environments where they can focus on quality versus quantity. They enjoy spending time in one place and do not need to fill up their days with tour after tour. **Extroverts**, by contrast, enjoy lots of activities, doing things with groups and other people, and meeting other travelers and locals. They enjoy filling up their days with events and activities. At the end of a busy day overseas, Introverts prefer to go to their room alone to get some peace and quiet, while Extroverts want to go out after dinner and spend the night on the town.

Sensers/Intuiters: Sensers enjoy observing and making sense of the world through their senses. As such, they can easily become overwhelmed when traveling abroad, especially in a chaotic context. Loud and active cities could be a challenge for them, and the same could be said for many other places such as India or Thailand. **Intuiters** are less impacted by their sensors and enjoy intuiting their surroundings. Because they do not take in their environment through their five senses, they are less affected by noisy and overly chaotic situations and contexts.

Thinkers/Feelers: Feelers enjoy making personal connections and value relationships. They are acutely aware of their own feelings as well as those of others. They enjoy opportunities to meet with others while traveling and processing their feelings. **Thinkers** enjoy getting to learn while traveling and take any opportunity to gain in understanding of their environment. They devour facts, discoveries, and quotes they come across when traveling overseas.

Judgers/Perceivers: Judgers love making decisions and getting things accomplished. They also like itineraries, schedules, and knowing how each day of their trip will look. Judgers have a low ambiguity tolerance, and they will have a hard time if their trip has no parameters or they do not know how to prepare or what to anticipate. **Perceivers** are much more flexible and do not need to know what they will do every day or how they will prepare. They are adaptable and can be spontaneous, recognizing that overseas travel cannot be controlled or perfectly planned. They prefer having open-ended plans on a trip so that they can decide in the moment what they want to do.

(2) Enneagram

The Enneagram organizes human personalities into one of 9 styles, desires, and dispositions. Each disposition, called a number or type, possesses a distinct way of viewing the world and responds to it based on underlying motivations and fears. Each number is marked by specific characteristics and habits, including virtues and vices. One of the things I love about the Enneagram is its brutal honesty; although no number is better or worse than another, each comes with its own set of challenges that must be managed to prosper in our relationships and in our understandings of ourselves. Each number also provides a pathway to growth, so that it is possible to diagnose a certain number as "healthy" or "unhealthy." If you would like to learn more about the Enneagram, there are numerous resources available. For websites, try EnneagramInstitute.com and EclecticEnergies.com; and for books, I recommend *The Modern Enneagram*, *Understanding the Enneagram*, and *The Wisdom of the Enneagram*.

Threes or Triads

The 9 numbers on the Enneagram are subdivided into triads. These correspond to 3 numbers connected to the heart, 3 to the head, and 3 to the gut. In short, the heart triad, driven by feelings, is composed of numbers 2, 3, and 4. While Twos are mostly concerned with the feelings of others, Threes are out of teach with their feelings, and Fours turn their feelings upon themselves.

The head triad, driven by fear, is composed of numbers 5, 6, and 7. These types plan their lives carefully. Fives turn their lives into one big intellectual enterprise, Sixes see the world as risky and even dangerous, and Sevens push fear away and concentrate on busyness, endless activity, and distractions.

Finally, the gut triad, driven by anger, is composed of numbers 8, 9, and 1. Eights externalize their anger to their wills, Nines run away from anger and hope it does not resurface, and Ones try to suppress anger by attempting to perfect themselves.

Each Number Briefly Characterized

As far as the actual numbers are concerned, below is an overview. It goes without saying that each one could be amplified and further charted into sub-types, uncovering a wide range of characteristics and motivations for each type. As such, take the brief descriptions below with a grain of salt.

1. **Perfectionist:** Critical, exacting, perfectionistic, likes things to be done properly and ethically with high standards, always seeking to improve, does not like to make mistakes and does not tolerate them in others.

2. **Helper:** Supportive, caring, defensive, dependent, desires to be needed and liked, concerned about others, defensive of others and sometimes possessive, finds fulfillment in serving others.

3. **Achiever:** Ambitious, driven, talented, success-oriented, image-focused, always wanting to be and do more, seeks validation, deeply concerned about success and appearance.

4. **Artist:** Artistic, creative, unique, introspective, dreamy, feelings-driven, needs to appear different from others, often turns inward and has difficulty conveying their emotions, enjoys the dramatic.

5. **Thinker:** Heady, intellectually curious, aloof, dispassionate, isolated, innovative, with a keen ability to assess and analyze, prefers theory over practice, likes to sit back and observe.

6. **Skeptic:** Likes rules, structure, clear guidelines, security, and safety, suspicious of things outside their sphere or routine, risk-adverse, needs reassurance, loyal to their leaders and loved ones.

7. **Socializer:** Fun-loving, energetic, easily distracted, enjoys the center of attention, loves hanging out with people and large groups, playful, likes variety, change, and new experiences.

8. **Leader:** Direct, confident, confrontational, autonomous, often has a take-charge attitude, rugged individualist, strong willed, protective of those under charge, aggressive to those questioning authority.

9. **Peacemaker:** Easy going, compliant, indecisive, likes to keep everyone or everything at peace, able to see things from many perspectives, does not like to be the center of attention or in charge.

Before You Go Overseas

Enneagram and Travel

When it comes to travel, the Enneagram classification system can help you simulate how you will respond to new situations, what kinds of trips you would find most fulfilling, how you will react when under stress, and how much tolerance you possess for the unknown—which is always present when traveling overseas.

Ones like trips that are planned perfectly, with careful attention to detail and purpose. They want to ensure that logistics are arranged efficiently and that every part of the trip is planned for a particular reason. They enjoy itineraries, guidelines, and explanations.

Twos enjoy trips that allow them to volunteer, help someone in need, or care for the environment. They are naturally others-focused and have a hard time pampering themselves. When traveling, they should consider at least one component that allows them to volunteer, give back, or help out the local community in some way.

Threes want vacations to accomplish something; they like to be pursuing a goal of some kind, whether it be touring every castle in Hungary, swimming at every beach in Portugal, or climbing every volcano in Costa Rica. They enjoy maximizing a trip to its fullest potential.

Fours are natural lovers of art, creativity, and beauty. They like being different and do not like doing "touristy" things. They would enjoy talking to a non-traditional artist and viewing his art, visiting a Bohemian neighborhood and having dinner with a local at her house, and checking out funky, off-the-beaten-path bars, cafes, and boutique hotels.

Fives want to learn when traveling. They experience the world through questions, frameworks, and ideas. When visiting a new place, Fives will want to do extensive research beforehand about a culture's history, beliefs, and sites. They are sticklers for facts. They are both a tour guide's pet student as well as her worst nightmare.

Sixes are concerned about security and safety. They do best in a location that offers little security risks and on a trip that lets

156

them experience the culture in as safe an environment as possible. They find safety in numbers, they cherish elaborate and iron-clad itineraries, and they like hotels with security guards.

Sevens are the opposites of Sixes when traveling. Sevens despise set itineraries, want to hang out with the locals, and are always looking for an adventure. They enjoy eating street food, learning a new dance from a local hangout, and taking advantage of every group activity offered. They are the kind of travelers that get lost because they wandered off (yet again) and lost track of time.

Eights relish a challenge, and their confidence in their abilities will usually serve them well. They like to take charge and do not want someone else telling them what they can and cannot do when overseas. They need some element of freedom.

Nines contrast Eights in many ways. Nines are easygoing and agreeable, willing to go wherever a tour guide or travel companion orders them. They do not like being in charge and will usually do whatever the group decides.

Figure 18.1 Travelers Respond to Circumstances in Different Ways Based on Their Personalities. Know Yours Before Traveling.

(3) DiSC

Created in the middle of the twentieth century, the DiSC personality profile measures four major characteristics: dominance (D), influence (i), steadiness (S), and conscientiousness (C). A DiSC test is based on twenty-eight questions that determine how you behave and interact with others. It is quite useful in the workplace, as it allows employers to simulate how you will react to specific situations and different personality types. If you would like to learn more, consider the websites discprofile.com and discpersonalitytesting.com. As for books, consider *Taking Flight* and *The 8 Dimensions of Leadership*.

Each Profile Briefly Described

Below is a short overview of each behavior preference.

Dominant Behavior	Brief Description
Dominance (D)	Direct, likes challenges, prefers to be in charge, strong-willed, confident, takes action, does not like to be questioned or under authority, wants to see results, values actions over emotions
Influence (i)	Optimistic, likes to collaborate and be around others, values relationships, enthusiastic and warm, likes to be popular
Steadiness (S)	Easygoing, good at collaboration, indecisive and prefers not to be in charge, wants peace and harmony, likes stability
Conscientious (C)	Enjoys learning and demonstrating knowledge, values quality work, analytical, critical, and objective, perfectionist, goal- and task-oriented more so than people-oriented

DiSC and Travel

You may want to consider the following when using DiSC for travel and international learning purposes.

Dominance: Those who score highest in D will want to be involved in a travel experience where they have a lot of control. Ds are direct, strong-willed, and opinionated, and they do not tend to do well taking orders from others. Ds need to do their own research and learn what they want out of a trip or learning experience overseas.

Influence: Those who score highest in I enjoy spending time with others, so they will want to maximize trips with friends, families, and groups. They will have a hard time traveling alone, so they should plan on having fun activities that will allow them to meet others and follow an active agenda. They also enjoy accomplishing tasks when traveling, especially when able to do so with others.

Steadiness: Those who score highest in S are closest to Nines on the Enneagram. They are accommodating, easygoing, and able to go with the flow. An S can find a way to have a successful trip in any particular context. Because they are so accommodating, though, they may want to consider choosing a trip where they can challenge themselves and make more decisions about what they really want.

Conscientious: Those who score highest in C tend to correspond to an INTJ personality on the Myers-Briggs. These types are intellectually curious, reserved, and approach life in a very systematic way, almost like a chess match. Cs enjoy a trip that allows them to learn a lot, to explore a new culture, and to have intellectually rich conversations with travelers and locals alike.

Conclusion

If you want to continue on the journey toward self-discovery, there is no end of resources available for free online or for purchase in a variety of formats. The three tools discussed, while some of the most popular, are certainly not the only tools available. There are a variety of assessments you can choose from, whether the Birkman Method, Strengthsfinder, or countless others. If you will be traveling with a group, having participants take one or two of these tests can be an extremely helpful and useful exercise. I sometimes require travel participants to take just one assessment—such as the Enneagram. The benefits are many. First, the results offer each traveler the ability to grow in self-awareness. Second, it gives me an opportunity to teach further on the Enneagram when in-country, where I am able to draw out specific examples and also make spiritual connections. And, finally, on long bus rides, while waiting at the airport, and at mealtimes, it gives travelers the ability to talk with one another and share more about themselves.

Reflection Questions

1. What kinds of tests have you already taken regarding your personality?

2. How might knowing you are an introvert or extrovert help you allot personal time on an international trip?

3. When it comes to packing and completing assignments like getting your passports, would you self-classify as a judger or a perceiver?

4. Out of the 9 Enneagram types, which one fits you best?

5. Does your workplace employ DiSC or use a personality test? Would you be up for taking a personality test before traveling with a group overseas?

CHAPTER 19
STAYING SAFE

Keeping Vigilant in Bolivia

We had flown into the capital city with the highest elevation in the world: La Paz, Bolivia. I had been to high elevations before, but this time felt different. Within a day of arrival, a couple of us contracted a clear case of altitude sickness. Common symptoms of this ailment include fatigue, light-headedness, shortness of breath, loss of appetite, and mental fogginess. We had all these symptoms, and after twenty-four hours of not eating anything (because we had no appetite nor strength to leave our rooms), we decided that we had to have a meal. We had located a convenient restaurant about a half-mile from the hotel, thinking we could walk there in about ten minutes. An hour later, after frequent stops to catch our breath and take a break, we arrived, not in the least bit hungry and physically weary to walk back to where we came. As we returned to our hotel, each of us holding feebly to our bag of food, a couple of street kids saw how disoriented we appeared and attempted to rob us.

You Are Not Invincible

For reasons I do not fully understand, many travelers think they are invincible and resistant to any serious mishaps. Personal experience, as well as hard data from the US Department of State, however, reveals that safety, health, and security can never be fully guaranteed overseas (nor domestically, for that matter). As such, the best approach we can take is to always stay vigilant and to follow many of the steps already discussed in this book regarding risk management, travel insurance, physical readiness, contingency planning, and cultural intelligence. This current chapter complements those items as there is much overlap. The more we arm ourselves with solid facts, achievable goals, and sound strategies, the better and safer the experience we are bound to have.

The ABCs of Travel Misfortunes

We will organize misfortunes that can occur overseas into the ABCs of travel misfortunes: (i) accidents, (ii) blunders, and (iii) crimes. Briefly defined, *accidents* are what occur unintentionally, *blunders* carelessly, and *crimes* illegally. Naturally, it is best to avoid all of them, but travel misfortunes take many sizes and shapes.

(I) ACCIDENTS

An accident is something that occurs unexpectedly or unintentionally. Although they can sometimes be prevented, they are not always anticipated (otherwise a savvy traveler would never encounter them). Unfortunately, serious accidents can and do result in death, and the following accidents cause injury to and even kill travelers every year.

(1) Automobile Accidents

In many ways, the safest thing you can do while traveling overseas is buckling up. According to multiple sources, automobile accidents are the leading cause of death among American citizens traveling abroad. Naturally, some locations are more accident-prone than others, but death by cars and buses are much more common than we would like. These deaths can occur while renting a car, riding in a car, and also crossing the street in a busy city. Because foreigners are unfamiliar with road signs (which are in a different language), traffic rules (which can be very different from one's own country), manual transmission (which is the norm overseas), and traffic patterns (which are unpredictable), it is wise to think twice before casually renting a car or before crossing a busy intersection.

Most Common Solution: Look twice before crossing a

street, walk among locals (not only is there safety in numbers but locals instinctively know local traffic patterns), and always buckle your seat belt (even if in the back seat).

(2) Drownings

Popular beach destinations like Mexico, Costa Rica, Jamaica, and the Bahamas contain the highest number of overseas deaths due to drowning. While most people naturally focus on the beautiful beaches and amazing climates these wonderful countries provide, the fact of the matter is that hundreds of people die each year due to rip tides, strong currents, and swimming while under the influence. Never assume that you are exempt from the hazards of beaches, lakes, pools, and rivers just because you happen to be on vacation or serving on the mission field. Water gives life and it also takes it away.

Most Common Solution: Never swim alone, never consider swimming under the influence of drugs or alcohol, try to swim in places with lifeguards on duty, and always obey safety rules. Never assume just because you know how to swim you can't be overpowered by unexpected currents, waves, and tides.

(3) Slips, Trips, and Falls

I don't think I've ever taken a group overseas where at least 1 person—usually more than that—doesn't slip, trip, or fall at one point. In the best-case scenario, all the person loses is their pride; but there are many worse outcomes that occur, including (i) scraps and cuts, (ii) bruises and strains, and (iii) broken bones or concussions.

Most Common Solution: Keep your eyes open at all times when walking, especially in places you are visiting for the first time, and be on the lookout for stairs, odd spacing between steps, and unexpected dips or drops in elevation.

(4) Food Poisoning and Upset Stomach

Most everyone who has traveled abroad has experienced the

intestinal discomforts of traveler's tummy at one time or another. This is the most common mild travel-related illness. It occurs when eating a bad meal or drinking water that was not sufficiently sterilized (including ice). Traveler's tummy, sometimes called travelers' diarrhea, is caused by bacteria, viruses, or parasites located in food or liquids that you consume. Not surprisingly, traveler's diarrhea is more commonly experienced by travelers in countries with poorer sanitation practices and poorer medical infrastructures. Common sources of foodborne illnesses are salmonella and E coli, which can cause anything from stomach cramps to vomiting to diarrhea to fever. In general, if your eyes or nose tell you not to eat or drink something, I suggest obeying them. On other occasions, use sound judgment and all your senses when ordering food, drinking liquids, and purchasing ingredients. And don't forget to wash your hands thoroughly with soap or hand sanitizer before eating or preparing food.

Most Common Solution: Stay away from questionable restaurants, be very vigilant of street food sanitation practices, never drink contaminated water, and don't overwhelm your stomach with new foods all at once (as much as possible, eat something familiar to your body each day). Eat foods that are well cooked and still hot and avoid foods that are undercooked and have been sitting out too long. Choose fruits and vegetables that you can peel yourself and be extra cautious when consuming beef, poultry, and seafood. Also, when visiting a new country, visit the World Health Organization (WHO) and Centers for Disease Control (CDC) websites for specific information about any health advisories relating to food. Finally, always carry anti-diarrheal medication such as bismuth subsalicylate (the main ingredient for Pepto-Bismol) as well as bottled water.

(5) Sunburn, Heatstroke, and Dehydration

Among my groups, I see this category of accidents quite often. Fortunately, it is usually a minor sunburn or a very mild case of dehydration, which can be healed by aloe vera and water and rest, respectively. As I mentioned in my chapters on jet lag and physical readiness, travelers routinely do not drink enough water, failing to remember that they are already mildly dehydrated the moment they arrive overseas due to not drinking enough water at the airport, low levels of humidity on the plane, and by drinking liquids that ultimately dehydrate you like beer and caffeine. When coupled with hours of outdoor activity and constant exposure to the sun, the results can, at best, wear you out and, at worst, land you in the hospital.

Most Common Solution: Drink plenty of water, wear sunscreen and a hat, and take as many breaks as possible when exerting yourself physically. Always have a bottle of water in a backpack or purse.

(6) Athletic Injuries

Many travelers visit countries overseas for the purpose of hiking, cycling, skiing, or playing sports. Injuries related to these outdoor activities are not uncommon, especially given that visitors are not as familiar with the terrain, climate, and new rules. If you are exercising or playing sports outdoors, acclimate to your new climate before being too active, always bring first-aid equipment, and consider not taking as many risks as you would at home.

Most Common Solution: Realize your limits and recognize that, even though you may be an accomplished athlete, there are hazards inherent to your new environment that you can easily overlook.

(7) Bug Bites

Travelers are especially susceptible to bites from bugs and insects like mosquitoes, spiders, and ticks, and they are not always sufficiently prepared for all the variety of new insects they encounter when overseas. If there are insects and bugs in your vicinity, act as if they will bite or sting you so that you take the necessary precautions to prevent that from happening. Bug spray, appropriate clothing, and monitoring yourself offer the best protection. Also, don't be fooled by how small an insect or bug may be; though tiny, they can be lethal. Mosquitoes, for instance, kills thousands of people each year in just a single bite.

Most Common Solution: Research ahead of time about what bugs or insects are prominent in your destination and bring repellent with you every day. Also, remember that long sleeves, long pants, and socks are sometimes the best protection against bites. At night, before going to sleep, examine your body for any possible marks, swellings, or bites. If encountered, treat them right away and consult medical care if they worsen.

(II) BLUNDERS

A blunder is a careless mistake someone makes. Everyone commits blunders—sometimes every day. It is part of being human, after all. However, when traveling overseas, we need to be especially aware of our weaknesses and limitations and not put ourselves in situations tempting us to act foolish, immature, or stupid.

(1) Over-the-Counter Drugs and Excessive Drinking

Illegal drugs, of course, are a crime and not a blunder, but there is a certain kind of tourism that gravitates toward legal drugs and legal drinking. You should never mix and match the two, and you need to be very cautious when doing either overseas. Avoid anyone who attempts to sell you drugs on the street. If you want to drink while traveling, only do so with friends you trust and who will not exploit the situation in any way. It's never advisable to drink alone or excessively. What's more, on a purely practical level, accidents you may experience under the influence of drugs or alcohol will invalidate any claims you think you have with your insurance provider. So, before you drink too much and end up doing something silly that causes an injury, realize that your insurance won't flip the bill.

Most Common Solution: Stay away from all illegal drugs and drink responsibly. Never drink publicly by yourself. Don't overestimate your ability to act sensibly while under the influence of drugs or alcohol.

(2) Animal Attacks

Figure 19.1 Do Not Be Like This Guy. Animal Attacks Happen All the Time. You Do Not Get a Pass Just Because You Are a Tourist.

Travel can make people more adventurous and willing to assume risks that they would not normally take. This can range from people being too carefree when on an outdoor safari, handling animals or reptiles that bite or are poisonous, getting too close to animals or creatures in the sea, and letting their curiosity of a new species encountered for the first time get the best of their judgement. Also, in terms of ethics and the law, many countries have restrictions on how people can interact with wildlife. If there are rules and laws in place (even if you disagree with them or think them excessive), do yourself a favor and just obey them and go about your day.

Before You Go Overseas

Most Common Solution: Don't handle, hunt, or feed animals unless explicitly permitted by law or under the supervision of a professional. Practice social distancing from any animals or creatures that appear aggressive, violent, or confused.

(3) Scams and Con Artists

Wherever there are steady steams of tourists, there are also con artists and scammers. The two go together like north and south, black and white, and right and wrong. The lengths that some scammers go to in order to make a quick buck off of unexpected travelers is legendary, and some scammers earn a full-time income by hoodwinking tourists of all kinds. There are many different types of scams performed overseas, so it is not possible to discuss any in particular. Some are legal and some are not. (Illegal scams will be treated below.) Some con artists are men, and some are women. Some work alone and some work with multiple members. Some are old and some are kids. In a word, scammers cannot necessarily be identified. They can be dressed like tourists, professionals, and anything in between. And even though they often work in pairs or triads, you will not be able to discern that from your brief interaction with them until it is too late. In general, and it's a regrettable reality, try to avoid eye contact with people when walking, and refrain from passers-by asking direct questions and thereby opening yourself up to a possible scam. Also, don't underestimate the finesse and ingenuity of scammers. They can be very clever, quick, and inconspicuous. Remember that some of these con artists are truly professionals.

Most Common Solution: Exhibit a healthy skepticism toward anyone who appears overly friendly, who invades your personal space, who approaches you with a direct question, or who wants to sell you something with a discounted price. In a similar way, always know where your valuables are and do not make any large purchases from someone who does not have a nametag or is not working inside a building or stand.

(4) Commercial Opportunists

Another common way people exploit travelers is through money exchanges. There are three ways this can occur: (i) money exchangers charge exorbitant fees or exchange rates, (ii) vendors take advantage of travelers paying in a foreign currency and thereby set high exchange rates for the local currency, and (iii) vendors return a currency that is no longer in use or is less than the agreed-upon amount. Among houses of exchange, those located in airports and in touristy areas tend to charge high rates for use and also provide exchange rates most unfavorable to the tourist.

When possible, and I recognize that sometimes it simply is not, exchange money in national banks that do not charge exchange fees and that offer equitable exchange rates. Also, when buying something overseas, it is usually best to do so using local currency; otherwise, you empower the vendors to charge whatever exchange rate they wish. Finally, when receiving change back from vendors, check it to ensure, first, that it is correct and, second, that you are receiving legal tender. If you are in Europe, for instance, where the Euro may be the currency, it is not uncommon for older forms of currency—such as the German Deutschmark, French Franc, or Italian Lira to still be circulating off the grid. Because travelers may be unfamiliar with the currency used in their destination—let alone keeping track of the exchange rate—you should familiarize yourself with the currency bills, coins, and exchange rates before you travel. Otherwise, it's very likely you will eventually pay too much, receive too little, or be taken advantage of.

(5) Non-Negotiated Pricing

With so much that a traveler has to keep track off, it's easy to let your brain go on autopilot when you enter a taxi or when a vendor approaches you and gives you a sample of something or offers to do something for free. In the financial world, there's an old saying that "there's no such thing as a free lunch"; the same applies in the tourism industry. Vendors, taxi drivers, and local entrepreneurs may appear casual and almost carefree whether they get paid when you first meet them, but, *after* you partake of their service or product, they can charge you whatever they want if you have not already negotiated and agreed upon a specific price.

Most Common Solution: Always settle on a price before you leave with anyone. If you are in a taxi, order the driver to use the meter. If you are riding an animal (such as a camel or donkey), negotiate the price before getting on.

(6) Selfie Mishaps

Figure 19.2 Selfies Are Great. But Never Lose Sight
of Your Surroundings When Posing for One.

Like them or hate them, selfies are here to stay. At every famous landmark in the world, every day of the year, selfies are taken by tourists of all background and nationalities. Over the years, I have seen travelers drop their cameras, slip on the ground, and be pushed over because they were not being careful enough when snapping a selfie. People who take selfies are also easy prey for pick pocketers to spot and exploit. Also, in a related way, be incredibly careful before asking a stranger to take a picture of you. The person you ask could very well be a tourist like yourself and happy to do you a favor, or the person could be a thief who takes advantage of the situation.

Most Common Solution: Take a full assessment of the area and circumstance before you take a selfie. Avoid precarious poses, and don't jeopardize your safety over a picture, regardless of how cool it will be. At the least, always encase your phone and protect your screen in case it falls. Finally, recognize that people taking selfies are standing ducks to thieves and scammers.

(7) Sexual Tourism

Sex in the tourism industry is nothing new. Each year, hundreds of thousands of tourists from around the world travel for the purpose of sex, pouring billions of dollars into the global economy. Sexual tourism comes in many forms, including, for instance, consensual sex between tourists, legal prostitution (it is legal in many countries), and sex between a tourist and a local person at a massage parlor, strip club, or certain kinds of hotels.

Most Common Solution: Avoid questionable establishments, keep aware of your surroundings and the kind of people nearby, and think twice before doing something you could regret.

(III) CRIMES

A crime is an offense punishable by law. Needless to say, you neither want to commit nor be the object of a crime anywhere or at any time, but especially in a foreign country that has less incentive to protect your rights and presume your innocence. Unfortunately, tourists are especially susceptible to crimes. In many ways, the moment you pull out a map, look lost, take pictures of a famous landmark, or walk out of a hotel lobby, you can pop up on the radar of a would-be criminal. In order to stay as safe as possible when traveling, you need to be aware of some of common ways criminals attempt to take advantage, exploit, or harm overseas travelers. What's more, it is important to become familiar with what researchers have found about crime and tourism.

According to criminologist Larry Seigel, for example, crimes are more likely to occur under one of these five predictors: (i) being in a high-crime area, (ii) being out late at night, (iii) engaging in risky behavior, such as doing drugs or drinking, (iv) carrying valuables, and (v) being alone (especially when combined with the other predictors).[2] Whatever you do, avoid these predictors as much as possible when traveling overseas.

(1) Peddling, Purchasing, or Smuggling Illegal Drugs

Illegal drugs move from country to country through travel, and unsuspecting tourists can sometimes find themselves being used or exploited by drug traffickers. Since 9/11, airports have done a much better job of patrolling potential offenders and criminals, but the drastic measures taken by airport security can never fully eliminate this threat.

Most Common Solution: Although it sounds severe, you should refrain from accepting gifts, watching personal belongings, or doing favors for strangers. Categorically reject any offers to buy, sell, barter for, or transport drugs.

(2) Mugging and Pickpocketing

Being pickpocketed or mugged is the quintessential crime that a tourist is always susceptible to. Tourist zones are magnets for pick pocketers, and these criminals earn a decent living by swindling unsuspecting travelers. In popular tourist locations, pick pocketers are always nearby, so never let your guard

2 Larry Siegel, *Criminology: The Core* (Cengage Learning: 2018; 4th ed.), 74.

down. I recommend only carrying one credit card and only cash needed for the day in a money belt under your shirt and keeping the rest of your valuables (including your passport) in your hotel safe. Never leave important items in your back pocket or in a purse or backpack. These can easily be stolen or robbed. Professional pick pocketers can remove these in a fraction of a second without you feeling or noticing anything.

Most Common Solution: Always be aware of your surroundings, don't let others invade your personal space, secure your valuables in a safe, and keep your money in a security belt around your waste that fits inside your clothes. Don't ever keep valuables in your back pocket or in a backpack. If it all possible, keep jewelry to a minimum.

(3) Identity Theft and Passport Fraud

In the technological age of the twenty-first century, many crimes have gone digital. Criminals can now steal your credit card, personal information, and other sensitive data without you every knowing—until, that is, they have spent thousands of dollars of your money or committed crimes in your name. Millions of tourists experience this misfortune each year.

When I returned from my last international trip in Central America, for instance, my corporate credit card provider notified me of suspicious activity and, thankfully, rejected charges that some criminal had made with it from Europe. I still have no idea how they obtained my credit card number, but that kind of thing happens very frequently. Passport fraud is also quite common in tourism; thieves can steal your passport information (even without possessing your actual document) and use it or sell it for criminal activity.

Most Common Solution: Purchase travel insurance, pay your bills at home (so that you don't have to so while overseas), keep your valuables stored in a hotel safe, do not enter any personal details or passwords while online (especially if the network is public), do not advertise your travel plans on social media, and notify your credit card or bank of any overseas travel intensions. When you return home, thoroughly review your credit card statement to verify that there are no unauthorized transactions.

(4) Human Trafficking and Slavery

Human trafficking is a billion-dollar enterprise and practiced in every country in the world. What's more, there are millions of slaves held and forced to work against their will in almost every geographic setting. In general, human trafficking includes the recruiting, harboring, or transferring of individuals by force or deception for nefarious purposes. The nature of trafficking varies from region to region.

In Cambodia, for instance, it can materialize as young girls being forced to work in massage parlors, karaoke bars, and beer gardens; in England, it can appear as children being coerced to transport drugs for gangs; in South Sudan, it can show up as a young boy being compelled to be a soldier in an illegitimate army; and in Ukraine, it could take form of women being abducted and sold internationally as wives. If you encounter trafficking of any kind, you must report it to a national human trafficking hotline or government agency (see contact information below).

Most Common Solution: Be on the lookout for suspicious behavior. Those who are being trafficked may have been branded or tattooed, display bodily injuries or signs of abuse, appear in emotional distress or traumatized, or be accompanied by someone who is older and more domineering. If you suspect human trafficking, the national hotline number is 1-888-373-7888 and the email address is help@humantraffickinghotline. org. Trust your intuition and avoid suspicious people. If you feel uncomfortable, go to a safe place immediately.

(5) Prostitution and Rape

Though surprising to some, prostitution is legal and accepted in many regions around the world, and it is a billion-dollar enterprise in countries like Germany. Some countries regulate the industry of prostitution and view it as any other profession, while others do not legalize it yet turn a blind eye to its practice. By contrast, rape is never to be permitted nor tolerated. Never force yourself upon anyone nor accept any unwanted sexual advances or attempts. When it comes to instances of rape, researchers have noted that persons who are intoxicated and alone are more susceptible to predators. If you are entering a country where prostitution is legal and culturally accepted, or where sexual practices are vastly different from your own, exercise extreme caution and judgment. In well-known touristy areas, solicitation for sex is common and certain profiles (such as single men or attractive individuals) receive more attention than others. If you find yourself the victim of unwanted sexual advances, report the incident to an official and find safety.

Most Common Solution: Avoid red-light districts at night, don't solicit or accept offers of sex for money or favors, don't drink or do drugs with strangers, avoid questionable establishments or neighborhoods, and don't ever go to a private place with a person you do not trust or know. Also, consider carrying pepper spray with you (or if illegal in that country, hair spray works) or wear a whistle around your neck that can be blown if you find yourself in an uncomfortable or dangerous situation.

(6) Kidnapping and Homicide

Homicide is highly rare among travelers going overseas. However, dozens are killed each year. Among Americans, Mexico is, by far, the country with the largest number of homicides. These are typically isolated to specific regions that fall within gang territories. Kidnapping occurs as well. The US

Department of State provides extremely helpful information about which countries pose the greatest risk of kidnapping, advertising the letter "K" on its travel advisory.

Most Common Solution: Avoid traveling to countries with a Level 3 or 4 from the US Department of State, especially when coupled with a "K" for kidnapping. Monitor local news and do not travel alone in any questionable locales.

7 Tips for All Travelers

All travelers who go overseas are susceptible to unwanted advances, travel hazards, potential dangers, and sometimes gender-specific attention or harassment. Rather than separate our discussion into different genders, ethnicities, and age, I thought it best to simply list 7 tips for travelers of all possible persuasions.

(1) Be Prepared for Unwanted Attention

Different genders and people with different orientations will attract unique predators, vendors, and opportunists. Depending on your gender and appearance, think about all the possible unwanted attention you might draw—for instance, solicitations for sex or drugs, invitation to people's homes or to a party, or verbal harassment and taunting—and determine how you will respond in advance.

(2) Know That Gender and Sexuality Roles Differ

In some countries, a solo female traveler is cause for concern; in others, it is completely normal. In some cultures, accepting an invitation to dinner is tantamount to agreeing to sex; in others, it means nothing more than having dinner together. Unfortunately, there is no way to know all the different cultural practices from one region to another, so it is important to remember that gender and sexuality expectations in one place may have nothing to do with what is expected in another. Do not assume that what is "normal" in your home culture is normal overseas. Perhaps it is, but perhaps it is completely different.

(3) Be Overly Cautious

Trust your instincts and do not get yourself into situations that make you uncomfortable. Be on full alert if you are in a sketchy neighborhood, if you are walking alone at night, or if someone approaches you that makes you feel uneasy or unsafe.

(4) Be Aware of Your Appearance

Hairstyles, jewelry, makeup, and clothing communicate a lot about a person. Be sure that you are comfortable with what you may be communicating to the culture in which you find yourself. If in doubt, try to dress more conservatively or, at least, do research about your destination and be aware of what is considered normal, typical, or expected.

(5) Always Plan for a Contact Person

Stay connected to friends or family back home and also be sure to always have someone in your location who is trustworthy that you can contact.

(6) Enroll in the Smart Traveler Enrollment Program (STEP)

STEP, as I mentioned in an earlier chapter, is a free program enabling US citizens to register their travel with the US Department of State. It is the best way to keep embassies and consulates aware of your whereabouts and able to communicate directly with you while overseas.

(7) Use Everyday Items as Self-Defense

When you walk around at night, take a whistle that you can blow if in any danger. When you go to sleep, place a doorstop in front of your door so that no one can enter. When you take public transportation, keep hair spray or a can of clothing disinfectant within reach if you are threatened in any way. Consider how you can turn everyday items into objects of self-defense if the need should arise.

Conclusion

Traveling overseas is one of the most exciting ventures that a person can experience, but it can also be a consuming and sometimes dangerous enterprise. Many people are on edge a few days before departing, anxious about their travel plans but also excited about what is to come. This may cause loss of sleep before your trip as well as stress, which is only compounded by jet lag and getting oriented to a new time zone once you arrive in-country. Then there are the spiritual and emotional toils of travel, which, unfortunately, can sometimes be combined with physical and safety concerns. As you travel overseas, consider all the accidents, blunders, and crimes that could occur, and devise a strategy that will keep you safe and secure while on the road.

Reflection Questions

1. What was the worst traveling mishap you have ever experienced on a trip? Do you think it could have been prevented?

2. How many of the seven accidents can you recall? Are you especially susceptible in one of these categories?

3. What blunder have you committed in the past that showed up on the list? Would you consider yourself a person that could be scammed?

4. Many people use social media as a personal diary. Why might saying when and where you are traveling be counterproductive?

5. Based on your age, gender, and other factors, what kind of predators may try to take advantage of you?

CHAPTER 20
ON PILGRIMAGE

Searching for the Sacred in Greece

We were in Patmos, Greece, a sparsely populated island in the middle of nowhere that ancient Romans used as a place of banishment—a kind of modern-day Alcatraz. According to tradition, a man named John wrote the last book in the Bible—titled Revelation—in a cave on this tiny island. The last time I took a group to Patmos, the group read Revelation aloud on the ferry ride over. Everyone got lost in the images of strange beasts, cataclysmic events, and gold-paved streets. Upon docking, the time you spend in the actual Cave of the Apocalypse is only a matter of minutes according to *chronos* time: "clock time." Because of other pilgrims eager to pay their respects to John in a place where biblical history was made, the Greek Orthodox priests overseeing the chapel monitor how long each person remains at the sacred site. But while groups enter and remain momentarily in the cave, where the smell of the sea is overpowered by the gust of incense and the darkness is extinguished by the light from small windows peering out into the sea, you are able to transcend time measured in minutes and find yourself deep afloat in *kairos* time: "eternal time."

A Pilgrim's Life

Traveling overseas as a pilgrim is one of the most ancient forms of tourism. It has been practiced for thousands of years. All world religions encourage this demonstration of devotion, whether Jews and Christians to Jerusalem, Muslims to Mecca, or Buddhists to Bodh Gaya. In fact, pilgrimage is a billion-dollar industry. Every year, millions of tourists flock to popular destinations like El Camino in Spain, Machu Picchu in Peru,

Before You Go Overseas

Varanasi in India, and many other places besides. Truth is, being a pilgrim does not mean that a person has to be religious at all. All that is required is a passport, a sense of adventure, and an eagerness to find meaning in an exotic land.

What Is a Pilgrim?

For those in North America, the word *pilgrim* conjures up images of black-and-white clad men wearing cone-shaped hats and women carrying baskets of produce. In the United States, the Pilgrims were a group of English settlers who established Plymouth Colony in the seventeenth century for religious freedom. Most famously, they are responsible for our nation's First Thanksgiving, which has since become one of America's most celebrated annual holidays. Although the Pilgrims were, indeed, pilgrims—that is, people journeying to a sacred or holy place for religious or spiritual reasons—they do not play any part in modern-day pilgrimage.

Pilgrims today come in all shapes and sizes: religious, spiritual, seeking, atheist, and agnostic.

I've met every kind of them on my journeys overseas, with some of the most spiritually hungry not professing to be religious or believing in God. This has caused me to expand my prior understanding of what a pilgrim truly is. I define a pilgrim as "a traveler in search of meaning, sacredness, direction, or connection." This definition necessitates three parts: (i) someone traveling (often overseas), (ii) someone actively looking for something, and (iii) someone acknowledging that certain locations are more spiritually charged than others.

If this describes your travel mentality, you are in good company. And you also have endless places to choose from. Today, there is hardly a country in existence that does not offer some compelling pilgrimage site, and some countries are world-famous for their time-tested ability to rock people's world with insight, energy, and illumination. Whether you want to pay homage to a legendary saint, worship in a sacred church, hike a solemn trail, or forge a spiritual memory, the world is calling to you. And, with it, meaning, guidance, and wisdom await you.

Your Framework *before* Your Pilgrimage

I will provide 5 interrelated frameworks to guide your pilgrim experience. They are all closely aligned and are not mutually exclusive. Focus on the framings that connect best with you.

(1) Between Heaven and Earth

There is a famous story about Russian envoys who traveled to Turkey in the tenth century to consider whether to adopt Eastern Orthodox Christianity as the state religion of Russia. Inside Hagia Sophia, the most grandiose church in the world that was built in the sixth century, they were overwhelmed with the church's grandeur and sheer beauty, confessing that "We didn't know if we were in heaven or on earth."

Figure 20.1 When Russian Delegates First Entered Hagia Sophia in Istanbul in the 900s, They Did Not Know Whether They Were in Heaven or on Earth.

This phrase gets to the heart of the pilgrim's dilemma: being pushed back and forth, like a game of tug-of-war, between heaven and earth. In the Middle Ages, when pilgrimage became increasingly common, pilgrims wore distinctive clothing and carried a staff and satchel to symbolize that they were "between worlds." This is what the word *liminal* means. Deriving from a Latin term that can be translated as "threshold," "doorway," or "doorstep," being a pilgrim is like pitching a tent under a threshold, never quite sure whether you are inside or outside.

This liminal existence is not easy. It is difficult to be a door that constantly swings both ways. Stated differently, although a pilgrim travels overseas seeking to encounter the splendor of heaven, we can only reach heaven with our feet firmly planted on earth. This reality can lead to confusion, disappointment, and misunderstanding. Spiritual moments, after all, are experienced in different ways at different times for different durations. No one can sustain them in perpetuity, and you never know when the spiritual high you are currently experiencing is going to land you back on the ground.

(2) Between Thin and Thick Places

In addition to the metaphor of heaven and earth, there are also other historic terms pilgrims have used to describe this mentality: thin places and thick places. According to author Mary DeMuth, "thin places are snatches of holy ground, tucked into the corners of our world, where, if we pay very close attention, we might just catch a glimpse of eternity."[3] They are places that are spiritually charged, but difficult to locate. Encountering a thin place is the goal of a pilgrim. It is like an archaeologist discovering a lost city from the past, a paleontologist finding the remnants of a fully intact dinosaur, and a detective deciphering the location of a hidden ruby. A thin place radiates spiritual energy and power, but it only does so momentarily, individually, and seemingly

---

3 Mary DeMuth, *Thin Places: A Memoir* (Grand Rapids, MI: Zondervan, 2010), 11.

arbitrarily. This energy strikes out in untold ways, and you cannot hold on to the power for long before it flickers away.

The opposite of a thin place is a thick place. This is not to be confused with a dark place, which is a place that has been tattooed by evil. Some of the darkest places I have visited, for instance, are the Killing Fields in Cambodia, where more than a million people were brutally murdered in the late 1970s, and Concentration Camps in Germany and Poland, where millions of innocent lives were taken in the 1940s. These are dark places. They feel as if they were animated by an evil spirit. However, a thick place is a wholly mundane experience, a place of spiritual stagnation, where nothing illuminating occurs even when you try to animate it. Unfortunately, two people can and do visit the same site and yet walk away with a different sensation. I have led countless pilgrim tours where, upon visiting a famous church or religious site, a few pilgrims encounter a thin place, several a thick place, and one or two a dark place. The life of a pilgrim is about searching for thin places, but also recognizing that thick and even dark places are encountered without warning.

(3) Between *Kairos* and *Chronos* Time

All this discussion of straddling heaven and earth and shuffling between thin places and thick places intersects with the notion of time. The primary purpose of your pilgrimage is to recharge your spiritual batteries, to connect with your religious heritage, or to find comfort in a power greater than yourself. This mindset is what the ancient Greeks called *kairos* time, "eternal time." It is time measured in eons. It is when your spirit becomes so enraptured in the moment that you forget all sense of worldly commitments. You become a weightless balloon floating up into the cosmos. But what goes up must also come down. All balloons eventually return to the ground.

Therefore, you have to come to terms with the fact that all

pilgrims face moments of disappointment, that some even get sick, and still others never find what they are looking for. This is *chronos* time, "clock time." It is time measured in minutes. It is when you get foot blisters from walking, disillusioned with a site you had always dreamed of visiting, and anger from being yelled out by someone in your group for spending too much time at a particular site.

Figure 20.2 Eating Lunch At This Beach in Patmos After Visiting the Monastery Is Always a "Kairos" Moment for Me.

(4) Between Divinity and Humanity

Indeed, for many, the most challenging part about a pilgrimage are the other people who accompany you. It is virtually impossible to stay on the same spiritual page as the others in your group, even if that other person is a spouse, friend, or church member. You may want to spend hours at a site, while someone else in your group prefers to simply take a picture and move on. Or, at night, you may want to pass the evening journaling about your incredible experiences and contemplating the places you will visit tomorrow, while your roommate only wants to watch TV and then go out for drinks.

The fact of the matter is that people will get in the way of your time with God. And that could be your greatest challenge on your pilgrimage. It is hard enough to maintain balance with our spiritual lives at home, so how much more so when overseas, when harboring unrealistic expectations, and when constantly surrounded by others who may get on our nerves and who have a knack for always saying the wrong thing at the wrong time. Regrettably, I have seen many spiritual moments shattered because one person was in a different state of mind than the other.

I remember one incident in particular. We were in Bethlehem visiting the Church of the Nativity, the traditional site of Jesus's birth. Returning to the bus afterward, one woman began sharing how meaningful the experience had been and how she will always treasure being where Jesus was born. The response from the woman next to her was heartbreaking. She said, "Yeah right, that place was awful. It was too crowded, it reeked of incense, and all I wanted to do was run out of there. They probably just made up that Jesus was born there to make a buck off of gullible tourists. What a joke." Don't be that person. Hold your tongue. Take an emotional thermometer check before complaining, criticizing, or condemning.

(5) Between Setbacks and Surprises

I have written in other chapters that international travel increases the chances of risk, disillusionment, conflict, and stress. No one wants to experience these things, especially during a pilgrimage. However, they cannot be entirely avoided. The life of a pilgrim is living between the disappointment of setbacks and the excitement of surprises. Let's not sugarcoat your pilgrimage. There will be moments when you will not feel spiritual, when you wish you were somewhere else, and when you would give anything to be with another group. But don't despair.

Although there will be setbacks, there will also be surprises. An unanticipated yet delicious conversation with a stranger, a moment of sheer serenity when you have total peace, or unplanned visit that turns out to be the most meaningful one of all. When on pilgrimage, lean into surprises when they come your way. They are divinely kissed moments that have the ability to make memories that last a lifetime. Ride these moments like a roller coaster, committing to staying with them until you arrive at the end of the way. As for setbacks, though, take them in stride. They will not last too long and owning and admitting that you will face them is more than half of the battle. Besides, surprises always outweigh setbacks. They are worth their weight in gold.

Your Practices *during* Your Pilgrimage

Although we go on pilgrimage to encounter the Divine, to seek for answers, or to get in touch with our true selves, most pilgrims travel with others, meaning that there is almost always another person standing nearby that will eventually irritate you, insult you, or just infuriate you. Of course, it's possible that your pilgrimage takes place alone, or your trip takes off without a hitch, but there are still several habits you can cultivate that will be worth your while.

(1) Journaling and Vlogging

I highly recommend journaling every day while on pilgrimage. I do so for three reasons. First, it allows pilgrims to frame their thoughts and feelings. After all, their brains and hearts are being flooded with so many ideas and emotions, which can be deeply overwhelming, and so they need an outlet to express them. Second, when reminiscing about your experience years later, it is surprising how much you can forget. However, having your actual thoughts and feelings on paper allows you to experience your trip in a whole new way. Reading a journal is like reliving the experience. Don't deny yourself this blessing. Finally, because most people are introverts, I like to give them an excuse for receiving needed respite from their extroverted friends or roommates. If you happen to be an extrovert, be sure to give your introverted friends time to process and, instead, seek out other extroverts. In addition, for extroverts, I recommend vlogging instead of journaling. It grants you the ability to process your experiences and have a memory years later, while also doing so in a format that works best for you.

(2) Net Effect

What exactly should you process while away? Everyone is different, but you should journal or vlog about whatever feels most urgent or whatever is on your mind or heart. I suggest spending a little time each day answering three intentional questions, assembled in the acronym NET: notice, energize, and takeaway. In my years of leading pilgrim trips, I learned that people need a simple way to frame their thoughts and emotions, and so this is what I devised.

1. **N:** What did you **notice**?
2. **E:** What **energized** you?
3. **T:** What will you **take away**?

I walk my groups through these questions every evening. We begin by reflecting on what we noticed. This can be anything, but it is usually something distinct from their everyday experiences back home. Next, we discuss what energized us. That is, we review what inspired us or motivated us in some specific way. For this exercise, I prefer to keep things positive, so I deflect negative comments that drag down the group. There is a time and place for that, but not in this space. Finally, I like for everyone to make a personal application. I encourage all travelers to take away something specific from their experience that day, whether a word, thought, feeling, mindset, or new habit they can develop. For those who do not know what to journal or vlog about, I encourage them to respond to these questions until they are comfortable processing something additional. And the great thing about the NET effect is that you can take your responses in any direction you like.

(3) Daily Examen

If you would like to go deeper with God on your pilgrimage, I recommend the daily examen (pronounced like the English word "examine.") The daily examen was popularized by the Spanish priest Ignatius of Loyola in his book *Spiritual Exercises*, originally written five hundred years ago. Ignatius was the founder of the Jesuits (officially Society of Jesus), a Catholic order active around the world today. The daily examen is a prayer of introspection and direction, and it is common for people to go through the prayer at nighttime. There are five steps to the examen, but the steps are not always done in the same order. When you begin, inhale and exhale a deep breath, find a place that is quiet, and get into a comfortable position. Your responses can come in any form: You could write them down in a journal or record them aloud on your phone. You can also do them informally by yourself or more formally with others.

1. **Gratitude:** You remember anything that you were grateful for that day: a delicious breakfast, the sun, fellow pilgrims, encountering a thin place, etc. A question to ask: What am I thankful for?
2. **Review:** Act like your day is being broadcast back to you hour by hour and moment by moment. As you observe what unfolded, consider what made you happy, sad, calm, angry, etc. A question to ask: What happened today?
3. **Sorrow:** Recall any moments that make you feel sorry. A question to ask: Did I do, say, or think anything that makes me remorseful?

4. **Forgiveness:** Your review of the day may have isolated an area of offense, compromise, or a misstep. Perhaps you made a bad decision, or someone offended you. A question to ask: What do I need to correct? Or who should I forgive?

5. **Grace:** You ask for the grace needed to do better the next day. A question to ask: Will you help me see and embody your presence better tomorrow?

Direct from the Source: Ignatius of Loyola, the founder of the Jesuits and the one who popularized the Daily Examen, ordered the examen in the following order: "The *First Point* is to give thanks to God our Lord for the benefits I have received from him. The *Second* is to ask grace to know my sins and rid myself of them. The *Third* is to ask an account of my soul from the hour of rising to the present examen, hour by hour or period by period; first as to thoughts, and then words, then deeds...The *Fourth* is to ask pardon of God our Lord for my faults. The *Fifth* is to resolve, with his grace, to amend them."[4]

If you would like to work through the examen while away, consider downloading the app Reimagining the Examen.

(4) Walking

Walking is one of humanity's most effective ways to process, imagine, and calibrate. There is something transformative that happens when you put your feet to pavement and lay bare your thoughts and feelings. It is not surprising, therefore, that walking and pilgrimage go hand in hand. If you think about it, many images of pilgrims from times past are of people walking down a path in search of meaning with a staff in hand. Jim Forest, author of *The Road to Emmaus: Pilgrimage as a Way of Life*, devoted an entire chapter to the practice of walking, writing that it "is a physical activity that is meant to have a spiritual significance,"

---

4 Ignatius of Loyola, *Spiritual Exercises and Selected Works* (Mahwah, NJ: Paulist Press, 1991), 134-135.

and that walking instructs us as "a school of wordless theology."[5] Walking is like attending nature's best classroom.

When I lead pilgrim groups, I try to always include at least one hike in the itinerary, and more if possible. This is usually quite easy to accomplish since many pilgrim sites were historically created for walkers. When walking, however, take to heart this medieval saying: "If you do not travel with the King whom you seek, you will not find him at the end of your journey."[6] Walking is always a valuable exercise, but it becomes a spiritual enterprise when you walk with purpose. As you walk during your pilgrimage, practice these three rules.

1. Pray, reflect, and savor.
2. Walk purposefully, remain clam, and be observant.
3. Monitor your breathing, lift your head, and feel every step.

In the end, the journey is almost as rewarding as the destination, so be sure to find joy in your walk as you also seek wisdom from above and around you.

Direct from the Source: Thich Nath Hanh, a well-known Buddhist monk from Vietnam, wrote a book on mindfulness when walking called *How to Walk*. One of his first pieces of advice is alarmingly simple, but it is rarely accomplished in full: "When you walk, arrive with every step. That is walking meditation. There's nothing else to it."[7]

(5) Prayer and Meditation

Depending on your own background and beliefs, the practices of prayer or meditation may or may not be part of your spiritual repertoire. Prayer can be done individually or corporately, and it is almost always present when groups travel for the purpose of pilgrimage. Groups oftentimes utter

---

5 Jim Forest, *The Road to Emmaus: Pilgrimage as a Way of Life* (Maryknoll, NY: Orbis, 2007), 7 and 11.
6 Forest, *The Road to Emmaus*, 13.
7 Thich Nhat Hanh, *How to Walk* (Berkeley, CA: Parallax Press, 2015), 10.

prayers or read scriptures when visiting specific religious sites. For instance, Christian groups that I lead enjoy reading and remembering Bible passages when visiting sites connected to those passages. We usually do this right before entering a site or on the bus if the site is busy and noisy. Meditation can also help clear your mind, calm your spirit, and recapture your balance when on pilgrimage. As with prayer, these activities can be done alone or with others. Meditation is about centering yourself and putting yourself in a place of peace, serenity, and openness.

Direct from the Source: Psalm 119:164 says, "I will praise you seven times a day." The so-called Daily Office is a set list of prayers that Christians pray every day. In the history of Christianity, there are seven Daily Offices that date back to the Middle Ages, which are distributed over the course of twenty-four hours. On a more popular level, the Daily Office is prayed twice a day: at *matins* (in the morning) and at *vespers* or *compline* (in the evening). The prayers are brief and set by the Church. If you would like to recite the Daily Office, you can read a *Book of Common Prayer* or download one of these apps: My Daily Office, Daily Prayer App, Daily Prayer, or Laudate.

(6) Spiritual Reading (*Lectio Divina*)

Spiritual Reading is an ancient Christian practice that seeks to unify the soul to God through the reading of Scripture. There are four steps, each representing a deeper union. If we liken spiritual reading to the metaphor of feasting, the four steps in parentheses are as follows.

1. **Reading:** Read a passage from Scripture slowly and humbly. (Take a bite of God's Word.)
2. **Meditation:** Reread the passage. Listen for the Spirit's voice as you focus on a specific word or image. (Begin chewing on God's Word.)

3. **Prayer:** Respond to God's Spirit by opening your heart in prayer and meekness. (Taste and savor God's Word.)
4. **Contemplation:** Reread the passage one last time. Allow the Spirit to work in your heart as you let go of the passage. (Swallow God's Word and let it digest in your body.)

Direct from the Source: The twelfth-century monk Guigo II wrote a book about spiritual reading. In it he explained that "Reading seeks for the sweetness of a blessed life, meditation perceives it, prayer asks for it, contemplation tastes it." (Guigo II, *The Ladder of Monks*)

(7) Spiritual Seeing (*Visio Divina*)

Spiritual Seeing is Spiritual Reading's cousin. It follows the same guidelines but, instead of Scripture, it makes use of an image or icon. Author Lindsay Boyer defines Spiritual Seeing as a "form of divine seeing in which we prayerfully invite God to speak to our hearts as we look at an image."[8] Spiritual Seeing is easy and natural to do on pilgrimage, since images and icons are readily visible and able to be purchased in gift shops. Spiritual Seeing can be practiced alone or guided with a group. Be sure to find a quiet space and pause between steps.

1. **Select:** Choose an image, photograph, icon, or piece of art. (Ideally, this should be an image you have seen on your pilgrimage.)
2. **Gaze:** Gaze at the image and be present with it. Be still, quiet, and attentive.
3. **Listen:** Allow it to speak to you. What is it saying? How does it make you feel?
4. **Pray:** When the moment is right, end the session and pray that this experience will positively shape your outlook and strengthen your devotion.

---

8 Lindsay Boyer, *Centering Prayer for Everyone: With Readings, Programs, and Instructions for Home and Group Practice* (Eugene, OR: Cascade Books), 30.

(8) Visiting Foreign Worship Spaces

It is hard to make a pilgrimage without visiting a foreign worship space. And even if you are visiting sites associated with your own religion, there will likely be regional or religious differences. Sites common to visit during pilgrimage are shrines, temples, churches, cathedrals, and other historic buildings and locations. For those who are attending a service from a foreign religion, it will take time to orient yourself to how a particular service is being conducted. Try not to rush things, have an open mind, and take a learning posture. Here are some questions to ask yourself.

1. What does the shape, location, and design of the building indicate about the religion and the people?

2. What is the first thing that caught your attention as you arrived and entered the sacred space?

3. How did you feel when you entered?

4. What was the focal point of the space? What colors, images, objects, or other things did you notice?

5. What are the main features of the service? Were any rituals performed, hymns sung, or books read?[9]

Architecture, incense, chants, vestments, interior design, the clothing of the people worshiping—all of these items shape your experience, and you will want to take in as much as possible when visiting a new place of worship. I remember visiting the Vatican for the first time. The property was immense, there were people praying, chanting, talking, and walking in every direction, and the exquisite detail of paintings, murals, statues, and buildings was overwhelming. When visiting a new space, slow down your pace, take your cues from others, and ask yourself what you want or need to learn from this experience, and focus on that.

9 Derek Cooper, *Christianity and World Religions: An Introduction to the World's Major Faiths* (Phillipsburg, NJ: P&R Publishing, 2013), 200-201.

Conclusion

Being a pilgrim is a full-bodied experience. All of your thoughts and feelings will be activated. Throughout your trip, you will walk, listen, pray, reflect, sleep, eat, laugh, tear up, get upset, learn, and wonder. People will experience sacred moments at different times and for different reasons. This underscores the fact that when you are on pilgrimage, you will constantly be straddling between different worlds, different time horizons, and different feelings and emotions. Regardless of how many spiritual moments you schedule, how many prayers you utter, and how many shrines you visit, this tension will frame your pilgrimage overseas, so it is important to give it full consideration. Fortunately, there are many practices that you can adopt while away that can offer you equilibrium and set you up for success, surprises, and illumination.

Reflection Questions

1. Did the definition of pilgrimage fit your definition? How did it overlap and differ?

2. What is your view of thick, thin, and dark places? Any other kinds of places you can think of?

3. What tips were given for journaling and vlogging? What is one reason it is so advantageous?

4. What is one other spiritual practice that caught your eye? Why did it resonate with you?

5. Are there any sacred locations in your daily life? Why might identifying a few of these lead to a healthier life?

CHAPTER 21
PROCESS TIME

Solace in Spain

We were just ending our journey to several European countries and happened to be staying for a few nights in Málaga, Spain. Nestled along the southern coast of Spain, and a short ferry ride to North Africa, Málaga is a popular destination for beachgoers retreating from the hustle and bustle of large cities like Madrid. As it turned out, we had found lodging at a beautiful retreat center overlooking the ocean with beautiful grounds to explore, a large library full of books to read, and interesting guests happy to share what they had learned over the course of their journeys. It was the perfect place and occasion for us to slow down, record our thoughts, and process our trip.

Your Trip Is Over, but Your Voyage Has Just Begun

It may be hard for you to believe that your trip is over. You may still remember the anticipation of traveling to an exciting destination and imagining all that you would see, do, and experience. You may look back in fondness when you think about the number of places you visited, the people you met, and the lessons you learned. Your voyage, however, has just begun. International travel experiences are like mental and emotional tattoos. Although your clothing may conceal it and you sometimes forget you have it, it will always be there.

Changing metaphors, you will most likely unpack your international experience over the course of years, with random memories flashing through your mind at the oddest and most unexpected of moments: while catching a scent of something that draws you back into another time, when watching a movie or reading a book and being reminded of a certain experience or feeling, and when daydreaming about nothing in particular and finding yourself plop down in the middle of one of the places you previously visited.

There Is a Season for Everything

If you are anything like me, you are still processing all your feelings and thoughts from your trip. The book of Ecclesiastes says, "There is a season for everything, a time for every occasion." It's been my experience that travel and change often go hand-in-hand.

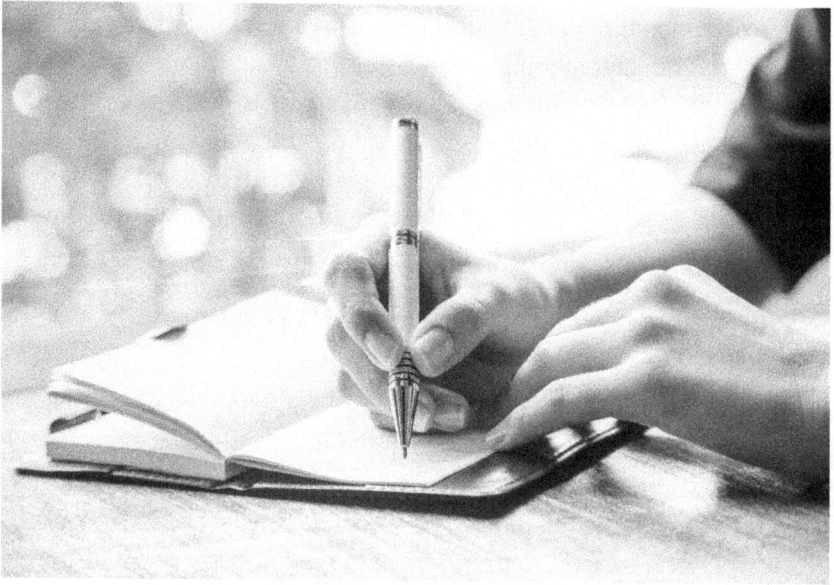

Figure 21.1 Journaling Is an Important Practice to
Do As You Process Your Trip Overseas.

During my years of leading trips, I've discovered that many people travel because they are considering a career or life change, and still others find that travel has provoked within them a yearning for something more, something deeper, something that will require change. Understood in this way, travel allows us to evaluate our hearts, questioning where we have come from and leaning into where we are going. What did you learn on your trip, and how will that change you in the weeks, months, and years to come?

There are many ways to explore these questions, but I recommend taking an honest self-assessment and working through the following steps and questions. There is no single way to process a trip, but it is absolutely essential to do.

Important Things to Do after Arriving Home

You will want to do the following when you arrive home.

- Journal or vlog your thoughts and feelings.

- Share your stories with family and friends.

- Do not overwhelm people with facts, stories, and rants. Tell your story in increments and shrewdly.

- Identify areas of growth. Write them down, think about how to build on them, and review them from time to time.

- Reflect on what you are to do with what you experienced and learned while away—both at the international and local level, both individually and collectively.

- Ask how you can allow this trip to positively benefit those around you.

Relax and Give Yourself a Break

"I never want to leave Portugal. I love it here!" "I feel called to remain in Vietnam. There is where I belong!" "I never knew Brazil was so amazing. I am going to come here every year for the rest of my life!"

I have heard it all. I have seen it all. And, without too much exaggeration, I have said it all. I cannot remember how many times I have heard travelers declare that they are never leaving their new destination, that they feel called to serve there, or that they are going to return all the time. These declarations almost never happen, and that is okay. Spoken in the moment, they simply represent our way of dealing with everything we have just experienced. International travel, after all, is a transformative and life-changing experience, and many people do not know exactly how to handle all of the intense emotions, breakthrough thoughts, and new life objectives that accompany it. If this happens to you, relax, and give yourself a break. Do not be too hard on yourself—or too critical of others who are overwhelmed.

Questions to Ask Yourself

Processing always entails questions that you ask yourself and respond to with honesty and thoughtfulness.

- What did I learn about myself?
- What did I learn most about my faith?
- In what area of my life do I need to grow and mature?
- What did I learn about the people with whom I interacted? What were my biases? And my fears?
- How has my perspective changed since returning home?
- What has been the greatest challenge since returning?
- In what ways did my culture enhance or detract from my time in a different culture?
- What is my responsibility toward others (faith, people you encountered, your group, yourself, your community, etc.)?
- Do I sense a new professional direction or renewal of a vision of what I want to do with my life?

Mission Achieved?

Most people travel overseas for a particular reason, whether for the purpose of vacationing, learning, or taking part in a mission trip or pilgrimage. Now is the time to assess whether you succeeded in accomplishing what you wanted to accomplish. Also, consider asking yourself what your future relationship is to be with the place you visited (if any at all). Perhaps it simply represented a vacation destination, and nothing more. Or perhaps it is a region that you want to visit more often and begin a partnership with someone or some institution there.

- Why did I travel overseas? What was my primary purpose or goal?

- Do I feel like I achieved that goal? Why or why not?

- What surprised me about the trip? Was the original purpose or goal of my trip altered in any way? How so?

- What role did this place represent for me?

- Who impacted my life there, and how do I want to stay in touch with them?

- Are there items left unfinished that lead me to want to return or build some partnership with the people or places I visited?

Revisiting Chapters and Questions

I have written this book specifically for you. Each chapter is designed to help you think through all the different components needed to travel internationally with success, happiness, and poise. You may have already read most of the chapters—either before or during your trip—and that is ideal. But there is also merit in reviewing certain chapters, reading through them again, and going over the questions asked in them. Your experience before or during a trip, for instance, can be vastly different after it.

Things to Keep in Mind in the Future

"Let's all get together in two weeks. We can relive all of our amazing experiences together." I hear this comment repeated after every trip, but it rarely pans out. In my twenty-five years of leading trips, I have never witnessed an entire reunion of travelers get together afterward. Despite our best intentions, there are simply too many barriers to groups recreating the special moments they shared abroad. People are too busy, people live in too many different parts of the country (or world), people have too many priorities, or the trip simply represents too many bad memories with the result that some have no intentions to seeing everyone again even after saying that they want to.

Nobody is perfect. We all experience things in different ways, and we should not expect more than is realistic. But here are some things you can do when you think about the other travelers you traveled with or met while away:

- Stay connected to your group and process your experience abroad with them. You can do this in person, on social media, or through texts, phone calls, emails, and video chats.

- Stay informed. Find different articles, blogs, books, websites, and movies related to the places you visited.

- Look for patterns or themes in what you learned while away. Follow up on them.

- Ask God to show you how to steward your experiences in a way that is edifying to others.

Conclusion

When returning home from an international trip, one of the first things we do is unpack our clothing and put it away. We then stow away our luggage, perhaps in an attic, basement, or garage until such a time as another trip may arise. It is a simple act that takes no special talent and can be completed in no time. Processing the feelings, thoughts, and memories of that trip, however, is a different story. And it will take much more time— and it will be much messier. Reflecting on your international trip is absolutely crucial because there are lessons trapped inside your emotions and ideas that need to be refined and released.

IMAGE SOURCES

Figure 1.1   Whirling Dervishes Ceremony in Turkey
Photo 118595808 / Dervishes © Simone Brambilla | Dreamstime.com

Figure 1.2   Tivoli Gardens in Copenhagen, Denmark
Photo 35212235 © Sean Pavone | Dreamstime.com

Figure 2.1   Millions Travel to Israel Every Year as Pilgrims.
Photo 22013067 © Yevgenia Gorbulsky | Dreamstime.com

Figure 2.2   "Travelers" Try New Foods When Overseas. "Tourists" Do Not.
Photo 57608755 © Thitikorn Nunbunma | Dreamstime.com

Figure 3.1   Before You Go Overseas, Have a Yard Sale to Earn Some Extra Cash.
Photo 25964486 © Joe Sohm | Dreamstime.com

Figure 4.1   Where You Stay Is Crucial. Read at Least 25 Reviews Before Booking a Place
Photo 13341433 © Tomislav Pinter | Dreamstime.com

Figure 5.1   I Recommend Every Traveler Purchase Travel Insurance.
Photo 27921200 © Cammeraydave | Dreamstime.com

Figure 6.1   Pickpockets Are Found in Every Country. Always Be on Guard.
Photo 34556257 © Ammentorp | Dreamstime.com

Figure 7.1   The First Time I Went to Quito, Ecuador, I Experienced an Earthquake. Natural Disasters Happen Every Day in Some Part of the World.
Photo 124811939 © Photosimo | Dreamstime.com

Figure 8.1   When Packing for a Trip, Follow the ABCs of Clothing.
Photo 81373668 © Khunaspix | Dreamstime.com

Before You Go Overseas

Image Sources

Figure 19.1 Do Not Be Like This Guy. Animal Attacks Happen All the Time. You Do Not Get a Pass Just Because You are a Tourist.
Photo 24107266 © Benkrut | Dreamstime.com

Figure 19.2 Selfies Are Great. But Never Lose Sight of Your Surroundings When Posing for One.
Photo 50658282 © Ocusfocus | Dreamstime.com

Figure 20.1 When Russian Delegates First Entered Hagia Sophia in Istanbul in the 900s, They Did Not Know Whether They Were in Heaven or on Earth.
Photo 26938079 © Wisconsinart | Dreamstime.com

Figure 20.2 Eating Lunch At This Beach in Patmos After Visiting the Monastery Is Always a "Kairos" Moment for Me.
Photo 156948741 © Nancy Pauwels | Dreamstime.com

Figure 21.1 Journaling Is an Important Practice to Do As You Process Your Trip Overseas.
Photo 57015929 © Karuna Em | Dreamstime.com

ABOUT THE AUTHOR

Derek Cooper is managing director of Thomas Institute, an educational travel company specializing in learning on location. He also manages Dodekagram, a spiritual formation organization designed for people living in a digital age. He is the author or editor of 15 books and has given lectures all over the world. He has visited more than 75 countries and earned a PhD in the history of religion and an MBA in entrepreneurial management. He additionally runs a YouTube channel called Thomas Institute. To learn more, visit www. thomas-institute.com.

www.ingramcontent.com/pod-product-compliance
Lightning Source LLC
Chambersburg PA
CBHW022018090426
42739CB00006BA/191